Marketing with Facebook and Social Media

By Bob Cohen

A bobology publication

www.bobology.com

Copyright 2023 by bobology. All rights reserved. Printed in the United States of America. Except as permitted under the Copyright Act of 1976, no part of this publication may be reproduced or distributed in any form or by any means, or stored in a database or retrieval system, without the prior written permission of the publisher.

Use of the methods, tools and techniques in this book in no way guarantees or implies any guarantee of safety from any harm, scams, frauds, or criminal acts that may occur to the reader's computer, data, or person. The information is provided as a means to educate and inform the reader of the options available for their own and their family use when using computers and the internet.

Throughout this book trademarked names are used. Rather than put a trademark symbol after every occurrence of the trademarked name, we use the names in an editorial fashion only for training and education, and to the benefit of the trademark owner, with no intention of infringement of the trademark.

This book is written with the understanding that bobology are providing information that is from sources known to be reliable. However because of the possibility of human or mechanical error, bobology does not guarantee the accuracy or completeness of any information and is not responsible for any errors or omissions.

bobology is a trademarks of Cohen-Naglestad Enterprises, LLC.

Class Workbook Edition

January 2023

INTRODUCTION

Topics

- Basics of social media and other Internet marketing

- How social media marketing works

- Using Facebook for marketing

- Facebook advertising

- Twitter, LinkedIn, Instagram, Pinterest, and Others

- Planning a Content Calendar

This book is organized to help anyone starting social media marketing, or anyone needing help advancing their social media marketing efforts. All social media marketing involves similar activities regardless of the social media involved.

This book and the corresponding class taught at community colleges is an introduction covering all the essentials for you. For more in-depth information, you can read these books or take the courses:

- Introduction to Internet Marketing Methods

- Search Engine, Google Ads, Email, and E-Commerce Marketing

- Blogging for Fun and Profit

- Content Creation in Five Steps

This book emphasizes using Facebook, the most widely used of all social media websites and an excellent place to learn how to use any social media site. I'll go into a detailed explanation of using Facebook and the marketing options available. There are others, and depending on your business, organization, industry, or market, some of the other sites and options may be more effective for your specific goals. We'll look at some of the options on the market today.

In this workbook, I cover the following topics:

- What is social media marketing – we'll start by looking at what social media marketing is, why it can help your marketing efforts, and how businesses, nonprofits, and other organizations use it.

1

- Content Marketing - using social media requires supplying fresh information (content) to publish on your social media accounts.

- Facebook Pages – since Facebook is the dominant social media platform in the marketplace, we'll closely examine how Facebook works to get a foundation that will prepare us for marketing using Facebook.

- Facebook Advertising – by creating a page for a business or organization on Facebook, it's possible to use Facebook to advertise and reach a targeted audience. I'll introduce you to how Facebook advertising works and how you can target specific groups of users based on their location, age, and other profile information that they entered into their Facebook user accounts.

- Twitter, LinkedIn, Instagram, Pinterest, and other social media sites are valuable ways to market your business. We'll look at the most popular social networks and what they can do for your marketing.

- Planning social media marketing – effective social media marketing includes putting together a schedule and a plan that focuses on accomplishing the most important activities. I'll give you tips you can use to start or improve your social media marketing efforts. If you're thinking of doing your marketing, you'll learn how to target your audience and determine the time and skills necessary for social media marketing. If you decide to assign the work to someone else, I'll give you tips on picking a qualified resource or contractor.

We'll go through each of these topics by the end of the book, and you'll be prepared to start your social media marketing efforts!

Why Social Media Marketing?

Why would you want to market your business or organization using social media? Whether you've decided to start or currently use social media for marketing, it's a business decision. It makes sense if your business or organization can increase sales, fundraising, customer satisfaction, or profitability using social media marketing. If you're already doing some form of marketing, it's valuable to understand whether social media fits your overall marketing efforts and where it can have the most significant impact.

Social media marketing focuses on developing word-of-mouth through people who spend time on social media sites. It's very much about what people say about you, not what you say about yourself.

Social media marketing succeeds in building an audience for your business's messages and encouraging your audience (fans, Likes, etc.) to spread the word about your business or organization.

When people use the internet, they spend more time using social media sites. In 2010, Nielsen (the company that measures TV viewers) estimated that the average Facebook user spent almost 7 hours a month using Facebook. To reach these users, you have to use the websites that they are using.

Search Engine marketing isn't going away anytime soon. People tend to use social media sites for social activities, and they use search when they are looking for something specific. However, as more people spend more of their internet time on social networking sites, marketers want to reach them when using them. To reach people, you need to go where they spend their time, and increasingly, that time is on ing sites like Facebook, Instagram, Twitter, Pinterest, and others.

The Marketing Cycle

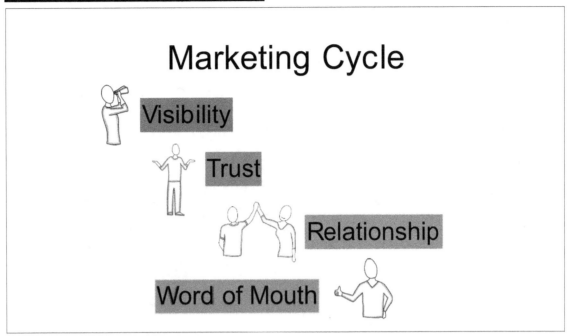

Internet marketing is a process with a cycle. This cycle consists of visibility, trust, relationship, and word-of-mouth.

Visibility lets potential customers find you. No one can do business with you if they can't see you in the first place. But being seen doesn't always result in people doing business with you.

A potential customer, or prospect, must trust you before he does business with you. Building trust by explaining what you do, why you're good at it, and using testimonials and references.

A prospect becomes a customer and establishes a relationship with your business. Market research estimates that you need as many as 17 contacts with a person before they become a customer. Customers are sources of repeat business, and the best companies continually communicate with existing customers.

A good relationship with customers results in recommendations, which leverage your customers to do marketing for your business.

Online marketers use web links and e-mail for this marketing cycle. Search engines work by using links to web pages and landing pages. The ability to use a search engine and click on a link that takes you to a particular website is a powerful tool, which is what Google dominates on the internet.

Email is used by almost every business to communicate with customers, especially after the customer makes an online purchase. Getting subscribers to opt-in and receive emails from you for a newsletter or promotions is a proven method of maintaining a customer relationship.

Social Networks Basics

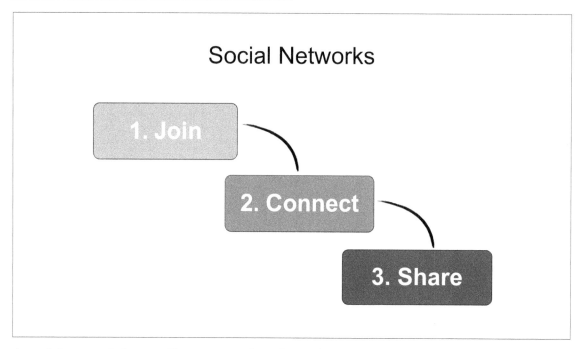

A social network is an online community of people or organizations who join the community, connect with other users, and share content and updates with each other.

Most people know social networks by their names, including Facebook, Twitter, Instagram, Pinterest, and LinkedIn, which are among the most popular social networks. After teaching classes on social networking (social media), I've determined that they have three characteristics in common.

What All Social Networks Have in Common

The three features of social networks are: join, connect, and share. Let's look at these actions and how they create social networks.

Join

To participate in the social network, social networks require a person or organization to join the site - by setting up an online account, usually through a website. You provide your email address and create a password. You may have to supply your name and one or two other personal information to create your account.

After completing this step, you'll receive a confirmation email, which is used to verify that you can receive their email communications. You activate your account by clicking on a link in the confirmation email. Now you have joined the social network and can use its features.

It's similar to joining other membership organizations you might know. A credit union is an example of a membership organization. It provides financial services to its members. You must become a member to take advantage of the services, for example, a checking account. To receive the benefits, you need to join. Credit unions have members, and the members have access to member benefits.

Since social networks are online communities, they use the web, apps, email, messaging, and other electronic communications to reach their members. Once you join, you have access to the capabilities of the social network, which are your member benefits. These benefits typically include connecting with other members and sharing information with them.

Connect

Since these are, after all, social networks, they assume you joined to be social, not anti-social. The whole point of a social network is to find and connect with other users.

Other users might be family members, friends, work associates, or a business or organization. Each of these internet users can have accounts on social networks. Ever seen or heard an ad that asks you to "Like" something on Facebook or "follow" them on Twitter? Asking to connect with potential customers is one way a company's marketing department builds a brand. Some social networks treat individuals and brands the same, while others have different types of user accounts—business or personal.

Share

Sharing on a social network is the way users let others know something. Users share their content with text, photos, graphics, and videos. Users share profile information, and Facebook has privacy settings that individuals can use to control who has access to certain profile information.

Brands share information about themselves similarly, posting updates, text, photos, images, and videos on their brand account. Facebook probably has the most differences between individual users and brands and has a type of profile called a Facebook Page that businesses, personalities, organizations, and even fictional characters can use. But sharing information on your account is pretty much the same.

Sharing content is more important for brands than individuals since the content a brand publishes can not only be seen by other users; the content can be shared. When another user on social media shares your brand content, their action spreads the content so some of their connections can see it.

As a result, sharing content on your brand account is essential for you to build a following and attract users.

Where Social Media Marketing Works Best

Using social media to create visibility, trust, and relationships is effective. Aggressive selling of a product or service on a social media site can work against you unless it's for special offers like coupons, discounts, or events. However, using social media to get a user's interest in visiting your site to purchase is a two-step marketing effort.

The reason is that social media users primarily socialize when using social media sites, not shopping, so they aren't in a frame of mind to look at a sales message as much as they would be when using search sites. Focus on the fact that a social media user does pay attention to what his friends are doing and what interests his friends have in activities, interests, and Pages.

Content Marketing

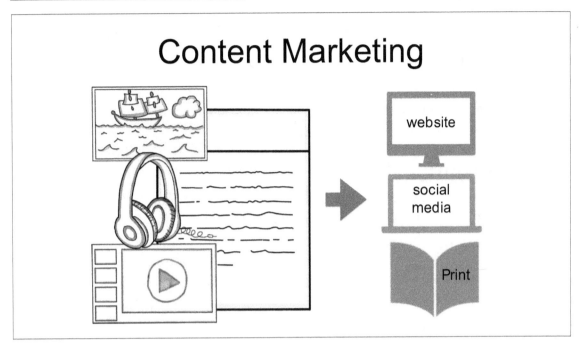

Why content publishing is important

Think of social media as a lure to get a prospect interested in your business or organization, with content that will attract her. Then, when she visits your site, you can establish that relationship and earn her trust to make a sale.

Social media marketing uses any social media site to reach the users of that site for marketing. In addition to being visible to a user, social media marketing leverages the users' contacts to spread information about your business. The ideal social media marketing effort involves users publicizing you to their social connections. Social networking sites also offer paid advertising options, and we'll look at the options later in the workbook.

Social networking allows users with accounts to share content with connections.

The phrase "content is king" is used because the content is the "product" people consume on the internet.

- Content can be any file or data usable online, including text, photos, images, graphics, video, audio, and links to other web pages.

- Connections are the relationships with other users that a person establishes with others.

Sources for Content

You are the best source for any content you post on social media. Any text, photos, drawings, or videos you create are yours; you can control how that content represents you. A content strategy is essential, and we'll look at some tools that allow you to schedule your publishing.

You can hire people from various sources if you're not a writer, photographer, graphic artist, or videographer. I cover content creation and resources in my Content Creation in Five Steps class and accompanying workbook.

Content Ideas

Active social media users share exciting and appealing content that they feel comfortable sharing with their social network on the internet.

Appealing Content

Giving users of social media sites a reason for connecting (or Liking) with you is crucial. Ask yourself the following questions:

- Why should they care about your business or organization?
- What benefit will they get from Liking, following, or connecting with you?
- Why would they check-in at your location?

Creating content that users will read, videos they will watch, photos they would want to look at, and posts need to be valuable and beneficial for the user. Organizations focusing on content have been the most effective at leveraging social media marketing to achieve their goals. Since everyone using social media has an audience (their network of friends, etc.), your message is viewed by the person you connect with and their audience (which is made up of them).

Stories

You've heard the saying that a picture is worth a thousand words, which is another way of saying that a picture *can* tell a story. The problem is that not all images are worth a thousand words. Some pictures tell a story and attract people who want to gaze at them, while others get a glance and are dismissed quickly. With so much content on social media, telling a story can help you stand out. And there are some simple ways to create a story.

A story can be written, a photo, a video, or a combination of all three. The important thing about a story is that it isn't just information; it connects with people. Helpful information is often static. It doesn't help people become engaged. A story turns knowledge into a narrative with a character or person the reader can connect with.

You might be a better storyteller than you think. Think about the last time you explained something to a prospect or customer using another customer experience as a story. The information is helpful but not that interesting. Saying "customers ended up with more business, happiness, etc." helps explain a result. Or you could say, "Mary, who was struggling with her social media marketing, started getting better results and more sales of her homemade candles after taking the "Marketing with Facebook and Social Media" class from Bob Cohen.

Don't misrepresent yourself, but stories about you, how people use your products or services, and how you make a difference with others are more engaging.

It's OK to Promote

Unlike a direct message aimed at a user to take action, the most effective posts for social media are aimed at building and strengthening the connection between you, your audience, and their audience.

This process, called "engagement," means that you can develop an audience for your business or organization by providing valuable and exciting content that your connections will spread to their network and your word-of-mouth marketing starts to work for you.

SOCIAL MEDIA STRATEGY: ORGANIC

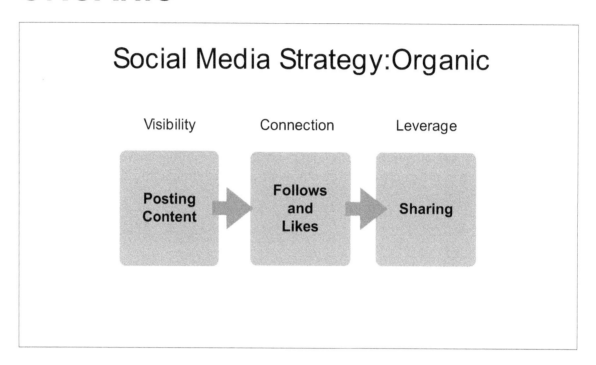

Leverage

To connect with any user on a social media site, you or your organization will have to become a site member. It's like renting a kiosk or retail location in a mall. Let me use Facebook as an example of this. Think of the Facebook Page for your business or organization as a store in a shopping mall. Your Page is on Facebook's "Mall." Just like finding a store in a mall, Facebook users can see your Page on Facebook, which has many Pages, just like a mall has many retailers.

You have an entry to your store (your Facebook Page). You might have a store window, signs with announcements, a sign that makes it easy for people to know who you are, and a display of some merchandise so people can easily see what you do and offer. These are your status updates on Facebook and other information about your business or organization on your Facebook Page.

Imagine if a customer visits your Facebook "store" and tells a friend about something he found. It could be a sale price, a unique item, or a specific service you provide. Now imagine that the customer tells ALL of his friends at once instead of telling just one friend.

That's what happens on Facebook. Your Page is your "storefront" in the Facebook "mall," and your customers and potential customers are your Fans. Your announcements are "status updates" and go out to all your Fans who want to receive your announcements as a

Social Action. When friends mention your Facebook Page, all of their friends hear about it on "Facebook."

Updates and Notifications

Social media sites allow users to share both static and updated content with each other. Static information consists of a user's profile, often with a photo and biography

that usually doesn't change often. Most social media sites use one or more forms with options for users to include biographical and personal profile information about themselves. This bio, whether short or long, is referred to as the user's profile.

Some social media sites want a small amount of user information, such as a name, location, and a short-sentence biography. In contrast, others, like Facebook, want to collect everything about a user. The profile could include a user's relationship status, work history, movie preferences, hobbies, books, sports, activities, and life events. A user's profile can be public, which is the case on Twitter, Instagram, and Pinterest, or shared only with existing contacts, such as friends on Facebook. This profile information rarely changes once aa user enters the data, which is why it's static.

Updated content includes status updates, posts, pins (Pinterest's name for updates), or tweets (Twitter). As a user publishes posts or updates, they become part of the user's history. The updates create the need for users to revisit the social networking site since there are always new posts from the accounts a user follows.

Social media sites also send messages on behalf of users. Called notifications, these are messages the social media site sends to a user, or their connections, when events occur. Some examples include the notifications sent by Facebook to a user's friends when they Like a page when a Twitter user mentions your username in a tweet, or when someone changes their job title on LinkedIn. Notifications increase the activity between and among users on social media sites.

Your brand or business must create awareness, establish user connections, and build an audience. Likes and followers are beneficial, but the real power of social media marketing occurs when your audience becomes engaged with your content and, through that engagement shares it with their connections on the social media site. When your audience starts to contribute to your social media activity, they become word-of-mouth marketers on your behalf.

Your Audience

Your Audience

- Who you're trying to reach
- What are their interests
- What do they like
- Why they would be interested
- How your product/service helps
- Describe your perfect customer
- Publish relevant content

Users are on the sites to:

- Socialize with people
- Keep up to date
- Find current information about a topic

Social media marketing is the word-of-mouth marketing of the internet. The goal is to get an individual's attention and make your message so appealing that the user is willing to share it with their social network. This user-generated content extends your reach beyond what you alone could accomplish. Targeting your audience involves creating a profile of what interests they have.

Delivering content your audience cares about will attract them, and they will be more likely to share it with their social network.

Some things you should learn about your target audience are:

- Interests
- Hobbies
- Relationships
- Location
- Family

- Travel
- Shopping
- Style
- Recreation

Use the audience characteristics profile sheets I've included to identify the interests of your target audience. The more you know about the ideal customer for your products or services, the more you can develop content they'll care about watching or reading.

Audience Characteristics Worksheet

Date: _____

Customer Profile and Characteristics

Is your customer a consumer or business? _____

For Consumers use Section 1A. For businesses, use Section 1B

Section 1A. Consumer/Individual Target Audience

Personal Characteristics

    Existing customers _____

    New customers _____

    Location or Distance _____

    Age   _____

    Sex   _____

    Income _____

    Marital Status _____

    Education _____

    Hobbies _____

    Sports _____

    Health _____

    Occupation_____

    Services Used _____

    Products Purchased_____

    Other _____

    Other _____

Section 1B. Business Characteristics

Annual Revenue _____

      Employee Size _____

      Industry/SIC _____

      Decision Maker Titles _____ _____ _____

      Number of Locations _____

      Geographic Target

            Global _____

            National _____

            Regional_____

            Cities _____

            Zip Codes _____

Section 2: Why would they use your product or service?

What benefits do they get? This will help you create the right content that appeals to your audience.

1. _____
2. _____
3. _____
4. _____
5. _____
6. _____
7. _____
8. _____
9. _____
10. _____

Section 3. Where and How to Reach Prospects

Prospect Touch Point - what media and activities will reach prospects and customers.

Publications read _____

Web Time _____

Social networking Sites _____

Popular web destinations _____

email subscriptions _____

Group memberships _____

Professional Groups _____

Social activities _____

Retail locations preferred _____

Classes/seminars/events_____

Home (phone, mail, etc.) _____

Office (phone, mail, etc.) _____

Trusted advisors (titles, occupations)_____ _____

Family members _____

Partnerships _____

Keywords searched _____

Ranking of Touch Points - Rank the top 4 approaches to use from above

1. _____

2. _____

3. _____

4. _____

Major Social Networks -Quick Look

Social Networks

 B2C - photos for fans to share

 All - Information, media, time-sensitive

 B2B - updates and group activity

 All - How-to, training, stories

 B2C - Physical item photos with links

 B2C - photos, design, fashion, travel

Here are the most popular social networking sites and the generally recommended targeting:

Facebook - a general-purpose site. If anyone uses a social network, it's likely to be Facebook. Best for reaching consumers or small businesses. Sometimes a group can be an effective way to build a community and attract people.

Twitter - a "newsy" and current information site. Used by the news media and experts in different industries. Twitter is highly timely and effective for public relations and establishing yourself as an authority on any topic. Also suitable for timely promotions since so many media users watch it.

LinkedIn - a business professional-focused site, LinkedIn allows users to build professional networks of contacts and keep up-to-date on topics in business topic-focused groups. Best place to use for business-to- business marketing.

YouTube - While not commonly regarded as a social network, YouTube is a popular video-sharing site. Users can like, comment, and share videos. If you can show something rather than write about it, you should be using YouTube. It's an excellent site for posting how-to and explanation videos and covers all demographics.

Pinterest is an idea-finding site that allows users to collect images from websites they find interesting and share them with other users. Most users say they are ready to buy something they like on Pinterest.

Instagram - is a photo and image-focused site. People like its visual content and the ability to discover new things. It has a younger demographic, but the content has to be visual. Fashion, style, and design all work well.

We'll go through each service's demographics and my recommended strategies for you to get the most out of each one.

FACEBOOK

Facebook

- Billions of users
- Most widely used social network
- Active users tend to be mid-life to older adults
- 90% of users outside U.S.
- Millions of advertisers
- META owns Facebook and:
    - Instagram
    - Messenger
    - What's App

Facebook is one of the most popular and versatile social networking sites. Originally started as a site for college students who had to have a college email address to join, Facebook did an excellent job connecting college students with each other.

Facebook opened itself up to all users several years ago, so now anyone can get an account and personal page on their service. It's one of the most versatile social media sites. It has always operated on the principle that agreement between two people is required to connect as "friends."

Facebook decided to allow other software developers to create applications using the Facebook website as a platform for their software which quickly accelerated Facebook's popularity to the world's #1 social networking site. Users have access to the functions and applications that Facebook develops and hundreds of third-party applications such as games, social activities, and software applications.

Facebook does not allow much modification of a user's brand Page appearance and enforces a consistent layout for all Pages. If there's one social media site that deserves your attention, it's Facebook, precisely because it's used by so many people, particularly in the United States.

Facebook's NewsFeed

NewsFeed

- Posts from friends appear first
- Posts shared by friends
- Ads
- Posts from Liked Pages
- Group activity
- Friend activity (likes, shares, comments)

Timeline is about you

Facebook allows users to share information with their network of connections, called Friends, using status updates. These status updates are text messages, photos, links, videos, or other content a user "posts" on Facebook. They end up in a location called the Timeline. A user's Timeline records their status updates and activities on Facebook. The Timeline is similar to a journal, but the nature of the content can be anything the user wants to post on Facebook. A post, or posting, is the process of updating a website. On Facebook, users " post" status updates of photos, text, links, videos, and questions.

NewsFeed is about others

When a user views her Home page on Facebook, it displays the NewsFeed. The NewsFeed shows her friends' status updates, some updates from Pages she likes, ads, and Facebook notifications about their Facebook network. Notifications are activities to a user that Facebook thinks are important. These messages can include information such as her friend's page updates, when one of her friends made new friends, when people accept her friend invitation, when someone's tagged her in a photo, and other messages that Facebook sends to keep her up to date on her social network.

Most of what's in the NewsFeed consists of information her friends publish. Status Updates can be text, links to websites, photos, or videos, and is a journal of the user's activity on Facebook, including any Check-Ins and Likes.

The Check-Ins and Likes are valuable for brands because users share the brand page with their connections.

Facebook automatically assigns a privacy setting for personal status updates (all brand Page status updates are public).

The personal status update box includes a black lock icon that allows a user to see the privacy setting for that post. Selecting the lock icon displays the current privacy setting and a list of available options for the user to change the privacy of the particular status update they are sending. A status update is only available in the NewsFeed of a user's friends. Still, it could be visible to friends of friends, the Public, or kept private to a list of friends, depending on the settings selected.

What's in the News Feed

When a user logs into Facebook, the screen Facebook shows them is the Home page for their account. Much of the content on this page is the NewsFeed consists of status updates from friends and pages. However, the order in which updates appear from top to bottom in the NewsFeed isn't chronological.

By default, updates appear in the NewsFeed from top to bottom in the order Facebook determines based on how much you interact with a user or Page. The updates that Facebook determines are most important to you use a formula based on the most valuable connections in your network. The method for ranking uses your activity with friends and Pages to determine the order in which stories (the status updates in your NewsFeed) appear, putting these posts at the top of your NewsFeed.

How Facebook Determines the Order of Appearance

Facebook doesn't reveal everything about how they rank stories. Marketing experts that follow Facebook agree on how Facebook prioritizes the importance of friends and Pages. Higher-ranking friends and Pages appear higher in the NewsFeed and are more prominent.

Facebook determines what activity from a Page appears in a user's NewsFeed using these factors:

- Recency – How recently a person interacted with a page. From fresh to outdated, the more recently a person interacts with a page, the more importance Facebook assigns to the page.

- Frequency – How often a person interacts with a page. For example, how often does a fan comment, like, share, or post on a page.

- Depth of Interaction – The type of interaction. In order of importance, these are Posts, Shares, Comments, and Likes.

Updates, Notifications, Engagement

Updates, Notifications

- People use social media to "socialize"
- They post content on their account
- People view content from their connections

Engagement

- Content is pushed when people:
  - Like or favorite an item
  - Comment (reply on Twitter) on an item
  - Share, re-tweet, or re-pin an item

Engagement occurs when you comment on someone's status update, send them a private message if they comment on one of your status updates, and do other activities where you would interact with a friend or a page. The more interaction there is between you and the friend or page, the more importance Facebook places on that relationship. Since the connection is considered more valuable due to the increased interaction, any status update from that friend or page will appear at the top of your News Feed.

For any social media, engagement with your fan base increases your visibility dramatically across a user's social network. Creating engaging content that invites and encourages comments, likes, and other interactions with your Page is one key to success.

Facebook has diminished the visibility of a Page's Status Updates in the NewsFeed of people who Like the Page to the point where only a small percentage, often less than 5%, of a Page's fans will see a Page's Status Updates in their NewsFeed. The reason is that Facebook sells advertising options for Pages to promote the brand.

Friends and Likes

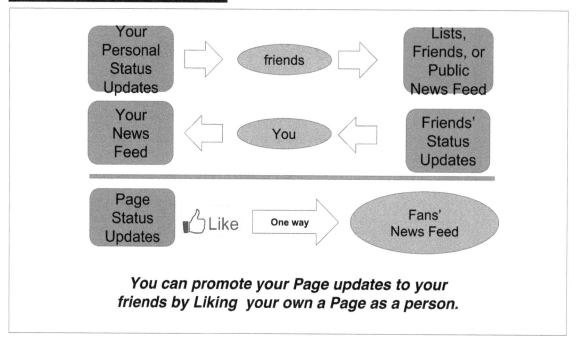

You can promote your Page updates to your friends by Liking your own a Page as a person.

Pages have "Likes," also known as "fans," while people have "friends." A Facebook user has a personal account used to create a profile, establish connections with people (who become friends), join groups, "Like" Facebook pages, and share information with their social network.

The information a Facebook user shares with friends is in status updates, photos, "likes," videos, interests, and other activities that Facebook sends out through automated notifications. For example, a Facebook user would create a status update by typing some text and letting their friends know they are taking a class on Facebook marketing. The status update is automatically sent out to their friends and will appear in the friends' NewsFeed.

User Profiles

Users on Facebook share their profile information with their friends and others based on their privacy settings. A profile is only as complete as a user has made it and may only contain a limited amount of information about the user. But the user can add additional information, including employment history, relationship status, sports teams and TV shows they like, etc. Advertisers on Facebook can use this profile information to target an audience. We'll see how when we get to advertising on Facebook later in the workbook.

Communicating with Fans vs. Friends

So you're probably wondering if I have a Facebook account as a person, why should I also have a business or brand Page? Remember what I described earlier, people have friends, and pages have fans. When using Facebook as a person, your status updates are shared with your network of friends and vice-versa. All your status updates use your profile photo and link back to your Timeline. You can use your account as a professional or to promote yourself as a brand, but there are some limitations to using Facebook this way.

Here are the reasons why:

- There is a limit of 5,000 friends for any user on Facebook. This may seem like a lot, but reach that limit, and you cannot add any more friends.

- You can't advertise on Facebook as a person; you need a brand Page to purchase and run advertisements.

- Your personal account only has room for personal information, which doesn't include a location for users to check-in.

- Places can have reviews.

- People can share any post from a Page since all updates on a Page are public.

Subscribing to Public Updates

A person receives status updates from anyone on Facebook through a feature called "subscribe." Subscribe allows other Facebook users to subscribe to public status updates on your personal profile without becoming friends. Any profile information and status updates with a privacy setting other than "public" will not be visible to subscribers. Using the subscriber feature is a practical approach for professionals in industries where the person is the business.

Status Update Visibility for Pages

When you post a status update on your page, not everyone will see it in their NewsFeed. Current estimates from marketing experts say that less than 5% of the people who Like a page will see any post from a page they Like.

When Facebook became a publicly traded company in May 2012, the company needed to show revenue growth for stockholders. Facebook has always given brands a free Page and allowed unlimited posting to the Page. Facebook's revenue is generated from advertising, so as it became a more popular social network, Facebook gradually reduced the number of Likes that would see an update from a page. By reducing the percentage of people seeing any post, Facebook encourages brands to purchase advertising to increase their visibility.

Differences between Facebook and other social media

While Facebook wants people to have personal accounts and brands to have a Page, other social media sites can differ. LinkedIn has personal accounts that can create a Company page, and company pages are used by individuals and organizations primarily for news and job openings. The other social media sites have accounts, and your account can be a business or personal one. You can have multiple accounts; they need a separate email address.

CREATING A FACEBOOK PAGE

In this chapter, we'll review the steps in creating a Facebook Page and the various content requirements. If you already have a Facebook Page for your brand, I recommend you still check the material in this chapter to be sure to complete any missing information.

Whats on a Facebook Page?

A Facebook brand Page is a like a website for your business on Facebook. It's free and visible to anyone, even users without a Facebook account. There are no monthly fees, setup fees, or other charges for any Facebook user to create a Page. There are no limits on how many Pages a user can make, and Pages can be created for almost anything. Viewers are required to sign up or log in to Facebook to Like a Page, but can still read any Page content without being a Facebook user.

In addition to businesses, Pages can be created for public personalities, organizations, brand names, websites, and places.

All Facebook Pages use what's referred to as the "Timeline" view. The home page layout is standard for all Pages on Facebook and cannot be modified, but you can add features.

A large horizontal photo, called the Cover Photo, appears at the top of the Page. In addition to the Cover Photo are the Profile image and the text name of the Page. A smaller version of the Profile Image, a thumbnail, is used with every status update. The Like button appears on the Page until clicked by a user, then it changes to Unlike.

Your page uses a layout that is managed in your Page Settings. You can reorder some tabs and add additional tabs from Page Settings and Edit Page feature.

Some tabs/sections cannot be removed:

- Home: always takes the user to your Home view

- About: more detailed information about the Page

- Photos: a gallery of all photos posted by the Page

- Videos: a gallery of page videos on Facebook

- Posts: shows the Timeline for the page

Additional links include buttons:

- Like: link for a user to like the Page

- Following: users can customize the way your posts appear in their NewsFeed

- Recommend: allows people to share your page as a recommendation post

- @pagename: a link to message the Page using Facebook Messaging

- More (three dots):

  - Save: users click to save or "bookmark" your Page with saved items

  - Share: share the page with a post

  - Write a Review

  - Create Page: starts the create a page steps

  - Like As Your Page: Like the page as your Page instead of as a person

  - Invite Friends

  - Block Page

  - Report Page

Depending on the Page settings, these links may appear:

- Message: allows users to send an email message to the Page via Facebook

- Call Now: displays the phone number

- Shop Now: uses Facebook's Shop feature

- Reviews: for pages that use the place category

- Locations: shows a map of sites for the brand

- Notes: displays any notes you created, useful for longer documents

- Calendar: any events scheduled using the Events feature

- Community: displays friends who like the page

Preparing Your Content: Ingredients

You'll want these things ready before your start creating your Page:

- Your business name for your Page

- Your Page URL name, the text that will appear after www.facebook.com, will be the link you'll use for any marketing.

- A photo or graphic you can use for your Profile Picture. You'll want a square image of equal height and width, and Facebook uses a circular image that cuts off the corners. A reduced size image of your Profile image, a thumbnail, is used whenever you post status updates and will be reduced for smartphones.

- A photo or graphic for your Cover Photo. This image tells your story. The more time and effort you put into your Cover Photo, the clearer your Page will be to visitors. Facebook does not allow the Cover Photo to use terms such as like, click, price, purchase information, or other promotional messages in the Cover Photo.

- Be sure to check the latest requirements for graphic image dimensions at Facebook's guidelines here: https://www.facebook.com/PagesSizesDimensions

- A short description of your business or page in 95 characters or less, including spaces. Only a few words of text appear below the Profile Image, and here is where you'll use your slogan, tag line, or short description of your business.

- A longer description about your business or page, but shorter than 50 words.

- You can add any specifics about your Page, goals, and purpose to the About section in a form for your Page.

- Your website URL, if you have a website for your business. You'll need the full URL, which starts with "http://." An example is "http://www.bobology.com"

- Your hours of operation

- A contact email for your business that can be displayed on your Facebook page (optional but helpful for people to contact you)

- A phone number for your business

- Your street address (which you will need if you want to use Facebook Places and Deals)

- Be sure to verify your Page to appear higher in search results on Facebook.

Steps to Creating a Page

Creating a Facebook Page

1. Go to facebook.com/pages

2. Enter a Page name

3. Enter a category

4. Add Profile picture, Cover photo, and About info

5. Claim the Page Name URL

6. Post content updates

7. Promote your Page

This section is for people who haven't created a Page or aren't sure if their Page setup is complete. If you're already using a Facebook Page, check the steps to ensure you've done everything for your Page to set it up correctly.

Facebook displays the steps and will walk you through the setup. However, I don't recommend doing any of the steps to promote your Page until you publish and post some status updates. You won't have any content and will promote a relatively empty Page.

You can skip any of the steps Facebook uses and go back later to edit your Page.

Set Up Your Page

Here's an outline of my recommended steps to create a Page:

Step 1. Go to facebook.com/pages

Start your Page at this URL: http://www.facebook.com/pages or any link that displays Create a Page. If you have a Facebook user account, you must log in; if not, you can create one for your Page use now. Many people want to create a separate account on Facebook to manage a Page. I don't recommend a different account except for an employee working at a company. Using your existing profile to log in and manage your Pages allows you to invite friends to Like your Pages. A single login makes using Facebook's mobile apps easier for managing Pages and personal activity.

Step 2. Enter Your Page Name

You are required to enter a Page name, but this can be changed at any time. Use your organization's name, business, brand, product, etc., in this text field.

Step 3. Select your category

Select a category. It can be changed at any time after you create the Page. Just start typing in anything about your page, and you'll see a list of categories you can select from to choose. The category you choose determines the type of information you can input to create your Page's Basic Information. For each category type, Facebook has a form for entering data. For example, a local business category usually has a physical address, so data entry fields are provided for entering this information. There are six general categories and many sub-categories within each one.

Any category that allows an address to be entered supports the Check-In feature so users can see your location on a map or get directions. You can also choose not to display your address in your About Page settings.

Step 4. Profile picture, Cover photo, and About

I recommend you complete the About section with information for your page, upload a Profile image and a Cover Photo, and complete any additional information about your business. Refer to the section on "ingredients" for photo dimensions.

Be sure to use words that describe your Page and make it easy to understand in a short phrase since any viewer will only see a few words. Think of this text as your "tag" line or slogan; if you already have one, use it here. If you don't have a tag line, now is a good time to write one. Visitors to your Facebook Page can click on the About link to see additional information about your Page, such as the location and other descriptive text.

For now, enter the short About description in the form provided. You can add more detail about your Page in the Manage Page link.

Profile Picture

After you select your primary and sub-category, you'll need to enter a name for your page, then accept Facebook's terms and conditions.

For your Profile Picture, it's essential to use one that displays well in the home Page size and in the smaller thumbnail size used when you post status updates on your Page. Similarly to a personal Profile Picture, this image is reduced in size and appears next to every status update. Because it's smaller, the thumbnail image may make icons, text, and some graphics challenging to read or understand. Remember this when choosing your Profile Picture.

The next step is to enter the About information. Some About text will appear under your Profile Image on your Page's Home screen.

Step 5. Unique Page Username URL

Claiming Your Page Name URL

http://www.facebook.com/

http://www.facebook.com/bobology

www.namechk.com

An important step is claiming a page name, URL, your page username. When you first setup your page, your Page is assigned a random or suggested URL that includes a username after facebook.com. A page name that reads something like mine, http://www.facebook.com/bobology, uses a specific phrase after the slash in the URL is claimed during your page setup. If you can't decide on a username, don't worry, you can change and edit it, which I'll explain in the Unique Username section below.

Facebook also uses your Page username with the @ symbol in front of it for messaging within Facebook. You can claim a unique Page username on Facebook at any time. Facebook provides this option when creating a new Page. A username is part of the Facebook URL after facebook.com and the slash "/" in the URL. A URL, which stands for Uniform Resource Locator, is the full address of a web page. It begins with the http:// and ends with the filename. Every web page on the internet has a unique URL.

Having your brand, business name, or a term that matches your domain name URL makes it much easier to give out your Facebook Page name to prospects and customers than the URL that Facebook assigns when creating a Page. Since web links are easy for people to use, just by clicking, choosing a unique Page name is more important for non-web media. For example, an easy-to-remember name will help people remember it. You'll be using your Page name more in print and other traditional media than on the web, so think about picking a Page name that is easy to remember and type in a web browser.

Once you select your desired username, you can change it only twice. If you need to change it again, you must create a new Facebook Page.

If someone already uses the username you want, you can't use it unless you have it trademarked. If you have a trademark and someone else uses it, Facebook has an appeal process. Since simple usernames are valuable in helping people remember your Facebook Page name, it's always becoming harder to get the one you may want.

Changing your username is possible by going to your Page and using the About tab in the left column. Click on About, and you'll see the Edit button to change your username.

Namechk

It's easier for people to remember how to find you if you use the same name on your social media sites. Luckily, a service can help you check if your brand name is available on Facebook and dozens of other sites. It's called Namechk, and it's free to use:

> www.namechk.com

Step 6. Start Posting

With the Timeline view for all Pages, the content on the Page is more important than ever. This content consists of the text, photos, videos, and links posted as status updates on the Timeline. I don't recommend promoting a Page until it has at least 12-20 status updates. Without this content, visitors to your Page won't have a reason to like your Page.

Step 7. Promote

Once your Page has some content with Status Updates, a Profile Image, Cover Photo, and a complete About section, you can start promoting it. Invite friends, customers, and others to Like your Page, continue to post updates, use other media, and use Facebook's advertising if you want.

Before starting, prepare your content so it's ready when going through these steps. By doing it "ad-hoc" or as you go through the steps, I've seen many people never go back and complete steps that they skip, resulting in an incomplete Page.

Ads

Facebook may offer you the opportunity to purchase ads to promote your Page during the setup process. I don't recommend advertising until your Page is setup and you have content with it. Advertising it too soon is like opening a retail store without stocking the shelves with inventory.

Status Updates and Posts

Focus most of your effort on posting status updates. After the Cover Photo, the status updates (posts) are what a visitor to a Page will see. High-quality and regularly posted status updates are a priority for any Page to be successful.

Create Status Updates/Posts

When creating a Facebook business or brand Page, I recommend posting about a dozen status updates before prompting your Page. Status updates are the single most crucial part of your Facebook Page content. Your visitors learn about your Page from your status updates, fans receive your status updates in their News Feed, and status updates create interaction with Facebook users. When a user likes, comments, or shares a status update, Facebook communicates the activity to the user's friends.

To post status updates on a Page is similar to posting status updates on a personal profile. Use the empty box with a message inviting you to share what you have been up to or what's on your mind. Click your cursor in this field to enter text for your status update. Type in your post, then click the Share button to post your update. Your status update is posted and will appear on your Timeline and in the NewsFeed of a small percentage of your fan base.

In addition to text, you can share a photo or video, a include a link to another web page. Sharing Links is a great way to direct traffic to an exciting website you find or to direct your fans to a site where they can get additional information. To share a Link, enter the URL in the text body of the post.

It's possible to change the date and time of a Timeline status update to a previous or future date and time by clicking on the clock icon. Privacy options for status updates are unavailable for Pages since all content is public, so you will always see the globe and the Public.

Photos and Videos

Photos are one of the most commonly shared types of status updates. Some market researchers have done tests showing that fans share pictures up to five times more often than other types of posts. Videos, posted in much the same way as photos, are popular on Facebook. However, research has shown that only a tiny percentage of Facebook users listen to the sound on a video (also try other social media services). I suspect that this is because most videos are watched on a smartphone, and the user may not be in a location where having the sound on is appropriate. If you use videos on social media, be sure to use a self-explanatory video or text annotations.

Posting Photos/Videos

Click on the camera icon to post a photo or video. On a desktop, you can upload a photo/video from a file. From a smartphone, you'll have options for using a photo/video from your library or taking a photo/video. If you have a Facebook Shop, you can tag photos to create links to your products in the Facebook Shop.

- Reels are vertical format short videos.

- Stories are posts that appear for a limited time and then disappear.

Tags

Facebook Pages can tag products if they use Facebook's shopping cart called Facebook Shops. A tag on a photo link to the Facebook Shop listing for the product will help it appear higher in search results.

Editing Posts

You can view all of your posts from the Manage Page view by scrolling down or selecting the Insights link, which gives you a view of all your posts and other statistics about your Page.

Other Important Posts

Several options are available for other types of status updates. These different posts are free to create but offer the opportunity to advertise, which is why they are separate from the standard status update post.

Click the More button, and a drop-down menu appears with options for Shop, Events, Offers, and additional items. Shop, Events, and Offers are the most important

Live Feed

A Live Feed is a video broadcast over Facebook. You'll need a webcam and a microphone connected to your computer to do a live feed. Once you start your Live Feed, it's available and public on your Facebook Page for anyone to view.

Live Feed can help you reach audiences looking for training and other information.

You can also connect a Zoom meeting to your Live Feed so you can use your Zoom account for a broadcast. To use Live Feed with Zoom, you'll need a paid Zoom account, but it's free on Facebook.

Jobs

Employers can post jobs on Facebook. Although not used as much as LinkedIn for job postings, Facebook offers the opportunity to reach a more diverse employment base.

Shop

Facebook gives you a complete e-commerce function with the ability to set up a storefront within your Facebook Page. Shops are currently limited to physical products. Facebook Shops allows you to enter product descriptions and photos and gives the user a complete checkout experience, sending you an order email to fulfill.

Facebook takes a small processing fee, similar to a merchant account, so the costs are minimal. Your products can be tagged in a post, so users can click on the tag and immediately go to your product listing page.

Events

If you have a promotion, seminar, or other activity that you want to tell your fans about, you can use the Event application rather than using a status update. Facebook statistics indicate that over 40% of US users engage with public events monthly.

Using an Event creates a separate page for the event on your Facebook Page. An Event allows you to send out an event announcement, request an RSVP and update your event information. Select the Event post in the status update box to create your first event. For future ones, the Event link in the left column of your Page.

To create an event, fill out the relevant information in the form that appears. Your Cover Photo is selected, but you can change the photo. Then complete the data.

Enter a name, location, frequency, and time. Select a category because this is used in addition to location and keywords to suggest events to people. The description is optional, but the more information you can provide to your invitees, the better the results you'll get for your efforts. Then enter keywords and select from the options that appear as you type.

Here are some additional features:

- Link your Event to an application like Eventbrite or other ticketing partners. Using a ticketing app, you can charge for attendance.
- Update your event with status updates.
- Share the Event on your Page timeline.
- Boost your Event with advertising options.
- Add a friend or Page as a co-host.
- Share updates during the Event.
- Use your smartphone to Go Live with video from the Event.

Events are useful for special occasions and activities but use them sparingly so your fans know that an event notification means something special. In search results, Facebook provides search options by topic or title and an Events Near Me search.

Users engage with Events by selecting what they're interested in or going. They can invite friends and share the event on their Timeline.

Users who receive event invitations can RSVP yes or no, and your event page will display the RSVP tally. You can also send updates about the event to the invited users.

Offers

If you have experience with offers already, your success can be used to promote one on Facebook. Here are some tips for creating offers:

People like discounts, and make them substantial. A 10% discount may be too small on a $10 item, but it means more on something costing $1000. Try using a percentage discount and a price discount to see which offer produces better results.

Good images attract attention. Facebook advises Page owners to feature pictures of people using a product rather than just the product itself. Logos don't perform as well and aren't necessary since your profile picture will appear next to the offer.

Be sure to give people enough time to redeem the offer and set an expiration date that allows people to take advantage of it. Facebook's advice for an ideal length of time is seven days.

Manage Your Page

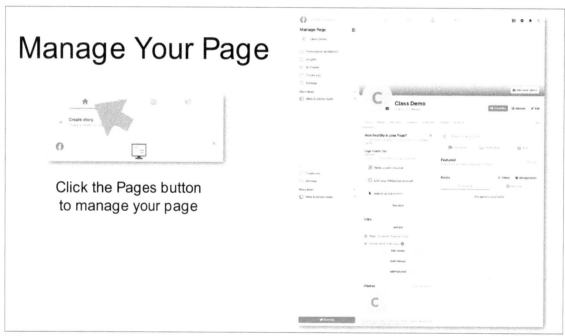

After creating your Page, you'll want to return to it to manage it with added content and advertising options. To manage your Page from your account, click on the Page button, a small flag symbol. If you have more than one page, they appear in a list.

After clicking on the Page button, the Manage Page screen appears. In this view, you'll see messages from Facebook about features available to you. And navigation links to areas where you can post content and manage other aspects of your Page. While it can see overwhelming, there are just a few important ones to pay attention to since the standard settings work for most organizations and businesses. Expect Facebook to make changes and additions as the evolve their software.

Important Navigation Tips

About

The About tab allows you to change and add basic information about your Page. Visitors will see information about your Page when they visit, so it's important to check this for accuracy and enter any information such as your products, services, and a description of your business or organization.

Ads and Promote

Facebook will display promotions for its own services, including ads. The Promote button will open the Ads view to start and manage an ad. Scrolling down will show more tools for your Page from Facebook.

Posts

There is a blank post box with options such as Live Video, Photo/Video, and Reel. Clicking in the text box will display additional post options on your Page.

You can also see your history of posts to edit, delete, or modify them.

Professional Dashboard

This link takes you to a screen where you can see insights and messages, manage your shops, and create events.

Notifications

Shows you activity by people on your Page, such as Likes, Shares, and Comments.

Insights

This view shows you statistics on your page's performance, posts, and other activities. Visit the Insights link often to know what content works best, what items are most popular in your shop, and more.

Settings

Access to options where you can modify your Page's standard settings.

Professional Dashboard

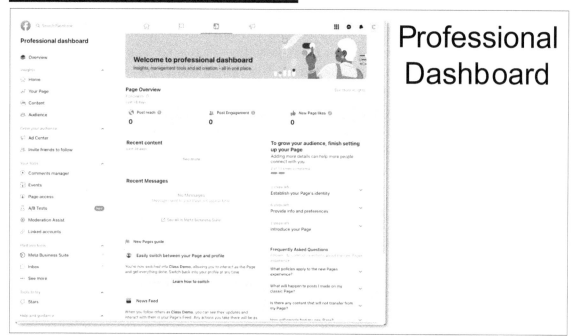

The Professional Dashboard gives you a view of your Page performance. You can also see insights and messages, manage your shops, and create events.

Linked Accounts

You can also link your Facebook Page to an Instagram account.

Inbox

You can see and respond to messages sent to your Page.

Content

Will show you the history of all of your posts.

Events

Create and manage your events.

Meta Business Suite

The Meta Business Suite shows your Facebook Page and connected Instagram account. You can use the business suite to manage and schedule posts for Facebook, Instagram, What's App, and Messenger, all Meta products.

Settings

One additional area is a gear that opens Settings.

There are many settings, but the most important are:

- Page Visibility - hides/displays your Page on Facebook.

- Visitor Posts - allows/prevents visitors from posting on your Page.

- Audience Optimization - targets an audience for your posts.

- Remove Page - deletes your Page from Facebook.

- Page Roles - where you can add other users to help manage your Page.

- Instagram - connect your Instagram account to your Facebook Page.

- Messaging - users can message you through Facebook, and you can add or remove the messaging feature from your Page.

- Page Info - add and edit your About information.

- Templates and Tabs - select a template for your layout and tabs.

Don't be afraid to click on any setting and its Edit link, which will show you the options and often includes a helpful explanation.

Facebook Help

There's no live help you can call for a Facebook Page, but two options are available on your Page.

- The question mark button in the upper right for help on any topic.

- A Help drop-down button in the upper right of your Page

- The Ask a Question button with automated answers.

- The Help Center in the Pages mobile app (tap the three bars in the upper left).

Marketing Strategy: Organic Content

The success of your Page depends on the quality of your status updates and the amount of interaction with fans (people who Like your Page), which is the engagement. Visitors who view your Page and users that Like it will interact primarily with your status updates.

With Facebook and every other social network, your goal with your posts is to build a following (Likes on Facebook) to achieve engagement with those users. When a user Likes or favorites your post, comments on it, or shares it, you've accomplished word-of-mouth marketing on social media.

Let's look at how to gain an audience, which consists of people who choose to Like your Page. Unfortunately, you're not the only one trying to get the attention of Facebook users and then click on Like. Creating a Page doesn't result in any marketing activity; it's the start.

Regardless of how a user gets to your Page, the value they see in your posts will determine if they Like you. Posting on a schedule that you can maintain and including content that will be of interest to users will encourage them to click the Like button. They will have opted-in to receive some of your status updates in their NewsFeed and added your Page to their Likes making it easier to find in the future.

There are many approaches to gaining followers organically (without advertising), and these are some ideas that will work with any social network:

- Add your Facebook Page link to your website

- Include your Facebook link in your email signature

- Post content that includes customers (with their permission):

- Photos of completed work - from hair to landscaping
- How-to guides
- Industry information
- Stories about your business and work activities
- Background about why you started
- News about your business
- Promotions or discounts
- Special events for social media followers only
- Ask people to Like your Page
- Answer questions from emails (remove personal information)
- Create a Poll post
- Ask for help from family, friends, and your personal network

These are just some ideas for posting content, where your efforts start.

To attract people to view your Page, which is necessary for them to Like it, you have several approaches:

- Inviting people you know to Like your Page on Facebook, which can include your personal friends on Facebook or an email contact list you already have for your business.
- Creating enthusiastic fans who spread your status updates to their friends with post likes, comments, shares, and check-ins.
- Purchasing advertising on Facebook to promote your Page.
- Using existing marketing activity to increase visits to your Facebook Page.

Let's review some of these now.

Building Your Audience

If you're already using Facebook, you are probably connected to some friends through your personal profile. Like any business or promotional activity, relying on your friends and family to help you get started can be extremely helpful.

Invite Friends on Facebook

One approach is to use the Invite Friends option from your brand Page. On the desktop view of your Page, click on the three dots (the "More" icon) and scroll down to Invite Friends. You'll see a list of your friends, and you can select the ones to send an invitation to.

Additional Methods

While inviting friends is a start, you must enlist other approaches to increase your Likes without advertising. These are some ideas I've collected from experience and other social media professionals:

- Include your Facebook URL on any collateral material.
- Use your Facebook link on your website.
- Place a sign in your retail location.
- Ask people to Like your Page in your email signature.
- Offer special discounts or offers available only on your Facebook Page.
- Train your staff members to mention your Facebook Page to customers.
- Give people a reason with your content to Like your Page and want to return.

The last bit of advice for increasing Likes is what every social media marketing pro recommends, post content that's useful and meaningful to your target audience.

Other Considerations for Organic Marketing

Remember that the key reason people use Facebook is for social networking. It's not a search site, a directory, or an index. People use Facebook because their friends, family, and other contacts can share news and activities about themselves with each other. Your marketing goal should be to create valuable and exciting content for your targeted audience. If your background doesn't include any experience developing content, now is the time to learn or consider hiring someone to do it for you.

Two comments come up most frequently from my conversations with business owners about their experiences using Facebook. The first is that they created their Facebook Page, but no activity exists. Often this comes from experience using a designed website that is never updated or changed. To make Facebook work, you must participate and join the social network.

Most brand Pages are liked by users because they find the information useful. You may have heard the saying "content is king," and it's true. You will have difficulty getting users interested in your Page without regular status updates. Regular updates don't have to be every day, but twice a week is adequate. Try not to go for long periods without updates, so your fans will always know that you update your Page and feel comfortable making comments. Ask your current customers what information they want to see and use that as a guide for your content.

The second comment I hear is that they don't have time to update their Facebook Page. They may know that it's necessary, but don't do it. Usually, this results from either not feeling comfortable about posting status updates or, as often as not, not having a plan for the content. Practice does help, as does setting aside some time on a calendar specifically for Facebook Page updates. Some users find that using an egg timer helps keep them focused on using Facebook for marketing and not getting distracted by using Facebook for personal networking. It's easy to get distracted. I know from experience.

You probably answer many questions about your business, products, services, or non-profit. Each answer is probably something that many people might also like to have answered, but maybe they didn't know what question to ask, or you were someone who knew the answer.

Use your business expertise as a resource for ideas to make status updates and posts on your Facebook Page, and you'll have more ideas than you have time before long.

PAID STRATEGY

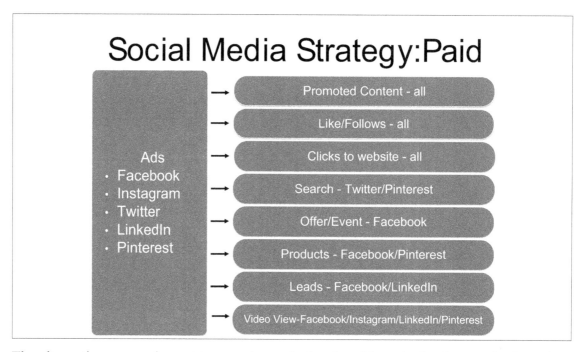

The alternative or supplement to organic marketing is paid marketing by purchasing ads or other promotional methods. Facebook offers the most options and features for advertising. But all social networking services can promote a post/status update, promote more followers/Likes, promote a video (if a video is supported), and run an ad that users can click on to visit your website. Some other ads are unique to the social network and are covered in the following sections.

Since Facebook has the most options and features and is the most extensive social network, learning about advertising on Facebook will make advertising on other social networks easier to understand.

Ad Types

I created this slide to give you a shortcut to the types of ads available on the most popular social media services. I've already discussed some ads on Facebook Pages, but this will give you a snapshot that will be useful to help narrow down your choices.

Promoted content
An ad that promotes a specific post, status update, or tweet to a broader audience. This type of ad is best used when you know your posts have engagement. If a post is liked, favorited, shared, or commented on, it's likely to receive more engagement if viewed by more people.

Like/Follow
This type of ad results in you receiving additional Likes (Facebook) or followers who will be more likely to see future status updates.

Clicks to website

One of the most popular types of ads since it results in sending the user who clicks on it to a specific webpage destination. It's the most similar type of ad on social networks to Google PPC Ads.

Search

Twitter and Pinterest are services where users can actively search for topics. Your ad will appear when users enter a specific search term, similar to the keyword search ads on Google.

Offer/Event

Facebook allows you to advertise any offer or event you create, so they are a separate status update type.

Products

Facebook supports product ads in Facebook Shops, while Pinterest supports an ad type called a "Promoted Pin." In each ad, a click results in the user starting a purchase. Pinterest requires that you use a shopping cart e-commerce service that is integrated with Pinterest. Two are Shopify and Big Commerce, which I discuss in my book and class on Search, Google Ads, Email, and E-Commerce.

Leads

If your marketing depends on being able to directly contact someone, a lead ad can be very effective. Facebook and LinkedIn have advertisements that result in you obtaining a lead with contact information rather than just a click on a website. Instead of using a webpage with a form to collect prospect information with a click-to-website ad, this is more efficient since you only pay for each lead.

Video views

If you have a video that explains a product or grabs attention, paying for views of the video can be a practical approach. You'll pay for video views, but you can sometimes include a link to your website in the ad.

Advertising Terms:

Before we get started going through the steps to create a Facebook ad, I want to explain some web and Facebook advertising terms. Suppose you've already done some online advertising. In that case, you might be familiar with some of the words, but Facebook sometimes uses them differently from what you might be used to seeing.

- Campaign – an ad or set of ads with a unique target audience. Facebook uses one ad per campaign, but you may come across advertising options where you can use multiple ads in one. An advertiser can run many campaigns. Each campaign has a creative (the ad that appears), a target audience, a duration, and a budget.

- Bid – the maximum amount per click or impression an advertiser pays for an ad.

- Impressions = # of times an ad appears - Facebook has options for buying advertising based on how many impressions your ad is shown. A user may or may not click on your ad, but you pay based on the number of times it appears.

- CPM – cost per impression, in thousands.

- PPC – Pay Per Click, a way of advertising based on the number of clicks an ad received and based on a bid price, or maximum, an advertiser is willing to pay for each click action.

- Click - when someone clicks on an ad.

- Clicks – the number of times your ad has been clicked on.

- CPC – cost per click - what the advertiser pays when someone clicks on the ad, usually an average since CPC can vary.

- Social CTR - Click Through Rate is the number of times an ad was clicked on divided by the number of impressions. For example, if an ad appears 100 times (impressions) and has one click, it has a CTR of 1%. Facebook adds the word Social to the description of CTR.

- Average CPC = Average Cost Per Click.

- Conversions = # of times a person takes action on the destination web page. If someone clicks on an ad to promote "Likes," a Like is a conversion.

- Frequency – the number of times each person saw your ad on Facebook.

- Connections: the number of people who liked your Facebook Page, RSVP'd to your event or installed your app within 24 hours of seeing this ad.

- Social Impressions – impressions shown with the name of the viewer's friend who liked your Page, RSVP'd to your event or used your app.

- Social clicks – clicks on ads with the names of the viewer's friends who liked your Page, RSVP'd to your event or used your app.

- Social Reach - people who saw your ad with the names of friends who liked your page, RSVP'd to your event, or used your app.

- Social % - the percentage of impressions where your ad was shown with the names of viewers friends who liked your Page, RSVP'd to your event, or used your app.

Facebook PPC Ads

If you've used online advertising before, you'll find this familiar territory with a few differences in social media. Don't worry; I'll explain it all to you if you haven't.

Advertising on Facebook has several options, and all advertising is paid. You can start advertising anytime after creating a Facebook page for your business or another purpose. However, I recommend that you ensure your profile is complete, upload some photos and a video, and create status updates so people who visit your Facebook page know what benefit they will get by liking it.

In addition to the Promote button on your Page Administration view, you can go directly to this link to learn about or create an ad:

https://www.facebook.com/advertising

Choosing a Goal

Facebook offers more ad options than other social networks. Two options available on almost every social network are an ad that increases the number of followers (Likes on Facebook) and an ad that promotes a post. Regardless of the type of ad, you pay when a user clicks, or with one more option available on Facebook, you pay per thousand impressions, regardless of clicks.

Before using ads, you need a goal, text, visuals that get attention, is easy to understand copy, and a destination link for the prospect when they click on the ad that matches your advertising goal.

The best ads ask readers to take a specific action and then take them to a page called the landing page, which follows up on the ad message. If you want more clicks to your website, use a destination page that lets them know what action you expect. A call-to-action is a task that you want the user to complete when they arrive on the page, such as downloading a file, filling out a form, purchasing a product, or booking an appointment,

Some Facebook ad types include a call to action, so you don't need your landing page. Some examples are the Lead Generation ad, where Facebook delivers the contact information to you from a form they provide. Another is the Offer ad type, where people can print a coupon or use it on their smartphone for redemption. These types of ads make Facebook easier for businesses to use. One type of ad you're unlikely to use is for an App, and let's see why.

Ad Set Name

A campaign is one or more ads targeted to a specific group of users. You chose those users to target based on the settings you selected in the targeting. Each ad you create requires a campaign name, called the Ad Set, so you can save your settings. The title will help you remember your settings for any ad you create.

For example, if you are a pet store, you might have a local dog grooming campaign, so you could call the campaign Local Dog Grooming. This will make identifying one campaign from another easier when reviewing your ad reports.

Automated Ads

Automated ads are a new option from Facebook, ideally suited to small businesses or new advertisers.

You answer questions about your Page and advertising goals, like reaching people locally or building more Likes. Facebook creates a few ads to try so you can see which ones will get the best results.

Facebook will take information from your Page, analyze your posts, search the people who already Like you, and develop an automated approach for ads that will adjust over time. You can start with an automated ad and modify it as you see its impact.

Boost a Post

As I mentioned, you should only boost or promote a post when you have one with some engagement. If no one likes, comments, or shares your post, paying to push it in front of others will not likely result in more engagement. Use your insights to find engagement posts, and then use advertising for one of those to see if you get the desired results.

Get More Calls

This ad will allow people to click to call you directly from Facebook. Us it when your sales depend on people calling you rather than visiting your website. Excellent for service providers, restaurants, and others who get business by phone.

Get More Messages

For example, if you want people to contact you through your Facebook page for a booking, this ad type can be helpful. A click on the ad results in people sending you a message to which you can reply. Unlike a lead ad, you can only communicate with them through Facebook Messenger.

Get More Page Likes

This is the ad type for getting more Likes. Likes are helpful since your posts will only appear in the NewsFeed of people who Like your Page.

Get More Website Visitors

The classic click to go to a website (webpage) ad. Typically most advertisers use this type of ad on Facebook since the ad can take the user to a webpage where they can make a purchase.

Get More Leads

This type of ad delivers contact information so you can directly contact someone who filled out a form.

Ads Manager

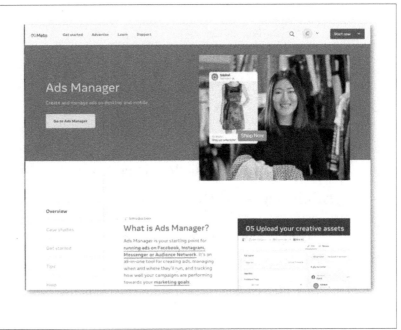

At some point, you may decide, or be directed by Facebook, to use the more comprehensive advertising webpage on Facebook called Ads Manager. The Ads Manager page shows steps for creating a new ad with campaigns in three categories; Awareness, Consideration, and Conversion. Each type has several objective options that offer a wide range of ad choices. Understanding your audience targeting and ad objective will make advertising easier to implement.

This is the link to start using it. Once you've done an ad or two, using Ads Manager isn't as complicated as it looks. Still, I wanted you to be aware of it in case you encounter it on your Facebook navigation. I'll walk you through creating ads using the Promote Page button, which offers a shorter list of ad types designed for beginners and lower-budget advertisers.

In case you want to explore the Ads Manager, here is the link:

https://www.facebook.com/business/tools/ads-manager

Some terms you'll want to be familiar with before using Ads Manager follow:

Awareness objectives:

- Brand awareness: reach people based on targeting and a call-to-action:
    - Website URL
    - Apply Now
    - Book Now
    - Contact Us

- Download
- Learn More
- Request Time
- See Menu
- Shop Now
- Sign Up
- Watch More

- Reach: increase visibility (impressions).

Consideration objectives:

- Traffic: clicks to a web destination on or off Facebook.
- Engagement:
  - Post engagement: promotes a specific post. Before using, make sure your posts get engagement (likes, comments, shares.)
  - Page Likes: clicks result in a Like.
  - Event Responses: promote an event.
  - Offers: get people to claim an offer.
- App Installs: get more app installs.
- Video Views: get more views of your video ad.
- Lead Generation: capture contact information for leads.
- Message: get more people to send you a message in messenger.

Conversion objectives:

- Conversions: uses the Facebook pixel (requires HTML installation on your website) to track conversions.
- Product Sales Catalog: creates ads from your Facebook product listings with targeting options.
- Store Visits: Use promotions and other options to driving visitors.

Promote Your Website

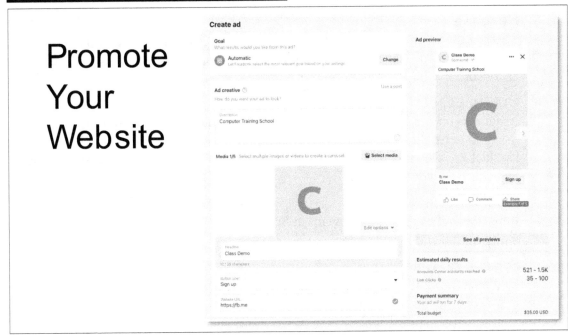

Let's use the most common type of ad on Facebook, Promote Your Website, since it helps explain all the steps and options available.

First, click the Promote button anywhere on your Facebook Page, then click on Promote Your Website. You'll see a view with some sections, so let's go through them.

Ad Preview

On the right, you'll see a summary of your ad, showing how it will appear to users in the News Feed. Click on the three dots to see how your ad will appear on a desktop/laptop full screen, Facebook mobile, or Instagram. As you change your ad on the left, the right column will reflect those changes.

Left Column

Ad Creative
This is the section where you change your ad's appearance.

Description
You'll need to complete the description text with your ad copy. You can only enter a short line or two of text as the space is limited.

Media
Facebook first pulls an image from your Facebook Page, which you can change if you prefer a different picture. You can use photos or videos already posted on your Page, and you have the option to upload a new image or video from your computer. Click on Edit Options to change. Photos can include text, which expands how much information you can communicate.

Using the Select Media button, you can also create a carousel of rotating images or videos.

Headline

The headline should be an attention grabber since it's in bold text and is the first thing people will read. It appears to the right of your profile image. All ads will display the "sponsored" icon so users know it's an ad.

Button Label

A button appears in the lower right of all ads. You have several options. Use the one most likely to get a click and tie in with your ad message. Some choices include Apply Now, Contact Us, Download, Shop Now, and more. A click on the button takes people to the website URL you enter next.

Website URL

Enter the webpage URL you want to link to when people click the ad. Be sure it ties in with your ad and is what people expect to see.

Special Ad Category

You must use this setting if your ad falls into one of the Facebook special categories with more specific terms and conditions.

Create Audience

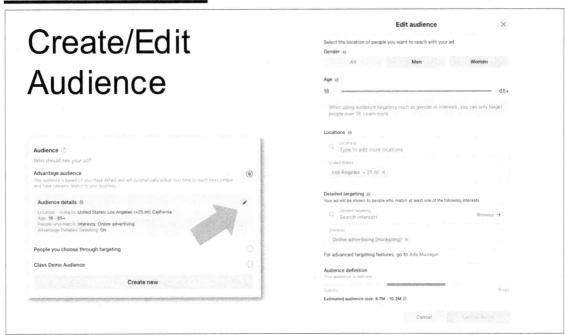

Most ad types include options that allow you to select which Facebook users you would like to see your ad. As an advertiser, you can take advantage of all the profile information that Facebook has collected from users and make audience selections so you target your ad to the right users on Facebook.

With the range of targeting options available for advertising on Facebook, it's possible to pinpoint your ideal prospect. The key to successful targeting is knowing as much as possible about them. Information about who they are, what they like, their interests, and their demographic makeup. Targeting your prospects enables you to spend advertising dollars to reach people who are the most likely customers.

Once you have created an Audience, it will be available for use in any ad campaign.

Audience Name

Enter a name that will help you identity the audience. Since all audiences are saved for use with any ads, it's helpful to enter one that enables you to recognize it. For example, Pasadena, CA 18-40 Men. So you can compare your results if you run the same creative to a different audience to compare results.

Gender

Select all Men or Women.

Age

Choose an age range or a specific age.

Locations

Everywhere in your country is the default selection. You can target based on people who live in the location, have recently been in a place, or traveling in an area.

You can include or exclude people by location, enter countries, states, and cities, or choose a distance range from a specific location.

Detailed Targeting:

This option can refine your audience based on demographic information, interests, or behaviors. You can target people who engage with Pages, the type of content shared, an app they use, interests based on what they view on Facebook, or the type of mobile device they use.

The targeting is based on what Facebook knows about a user form their activity on Facebook.

You can type in a topic, and Facebook will help by giving you a list of choices, or you can use the tabs to move through the options.

Demographic
Choose age ranges or specific ages, all genders, or only men or women. Languages can be selected, so even if English is the native language, you can still target people in a location who use a different language on Facebook.

Interests
Reach people based on their interests, activities, Pages they like, and other related topics.

Behaviors
This selection targets users based on their purchasing behavior, device type (iPhone versus Laptop), politics, and more.

More Categories
This tab is blank now, but watch for Facebook to add more selections.

Potential Reach

The Potential Reach of your ad estimates how many people on Facebook could see your ad based on your targeting. The number starts with all of your country's Facebook users and changes as you select each targeting option. Even if you only reach 5,000 people, it's not too small a number if they are the right target. You'll see an estimate of the ad results based on your targetings, such as clicks, Likes, or video views.

Using Targeting

Targeting options allow you to select specific audiences for your advertising campaign. Using any targeting option to reach Facebook users uses the database Facebook collects on every user when they use Facebook. As people use Facebook more by clicking links, Liking Pages, engaging in content, or browsing the web, Facebook learns more about them. The result to you as an advertiser is the ability to target ads only to people likely to become customers, provided you know what characteristics you should focus on reaching.

A lesson to learn from larger advertisers is testing ads and testing two ads against each other to compare results. It's possible to run two ad campaigns targeting the same audience but use a different ad for each campaign. Since the target is the same, you can measure which ad produces better results. Another option would be using the same ad but targeting different audiences to compare which audience yielded better results. Since ads can be created quickly and tested, this approach is well within the means of a solo or one-person business advertising effort.

Duration, Budget, and Placements

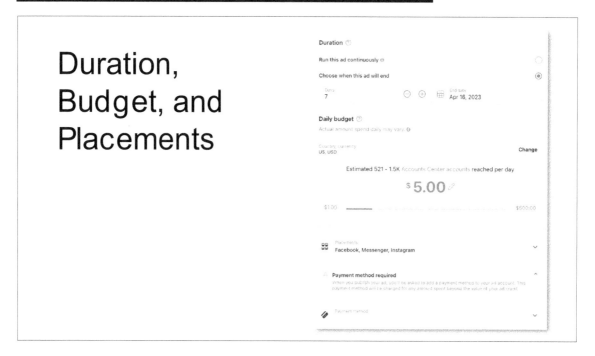

Duration

Under Duration, your options are continuous or set a period for the ad to run with a start date. Run my ad continuously starting today runs your ad after you click on the Place Order link and won't stop until you stop the campaign.

Daily Budget

You can set a daily budget starting with $1.00 per day. The budget is a daily limit averaged over a monthly period. But your fall spend may vary. For example, with a daily budget of $5, on one day, you might spend $6.50, but on another day, $2.00. Facebook will use the daily funding averaged over a month, so in a month, you won't spend more than $5 a day, on average.

As you change your budget, you can see changes in the estimated number of people reached daily. Your Total Budget is also displayed in the right column.

Placements

The Placements option selects the places your ad will appear. The Placement options are Facebook, Instagram, Messenger, and What's App. Depending on your Page type, you may be unable to deselect Facebook. I recommend leaving them all checked until you can analyze your ad statistics.

Facebook Pixel is a tracking tool for ad activity that takes people to your website. It's used primarily for conversion ads so website owners can track people's actions when they get to the clicked webpage. You must use Ads Manager to setup the Facebook Pixel to track conversions.

You'll need to enter a payment method, then your ad will be reviewed and it will start running.

Some Other Things to Consider

One good thing about internet advertising is that it's all managed. Your daily or lifetime spending will not exceed your budget, and you can start or stop the ad anytime.

If you remember from the advertising terms described earlier, Pay Per Click (PPC) advertising only requires paying when a user clicks on your ad. You set a bid price for the maximum you will pay for each click. Facebook manages the bidding so that your ad is likely to display often enough for it to use your daily budget. Facebook makes money when a user clicks on ads, so it's in their interest to show the ad often enough to spend the budget.

For campaigns that promote Likes for your Page, Facebook will list the estimated number of Likes for your campaign. With a Like ad, a click results in a Like.

I recommend using Facebook's suggested bid during the first two weeks of your campaign. You won't pay more than your maximum bid and daily spend selections. Remember, you are setting a maximum, often paying less per click than the maximum if other advertisers bid less.

Ad Copy and Design Can Lower Costs

However, ad copy and design can affect how often your ad is displayed. Some ads will get more clicks based on the content, topic, and visuals. Facebook only makes money with a click (except for impression ads). Facebook manages the display, so ads that are clicked more frequently are displayed more often.

This means that the ad with the highest bid isn't always displayed the most often. The quality of the ad and whether people click on it when it appears will affect how often Facebook shows the ad.

Tip: Before you bid more or increase your budget for an ad, try a different ad copy, image, or target. Be sure to change one item at a time to see what makes a difference.

Ad Reports

Facebook provides reporting for your ad campaigns in Manage Ads. There are two tools to analyze your ad performance: Facebook Analytics and Ads Manager.

Analytics shows the information on the audience demographics, devices used, and the source or ad funnel. Ads Manager shows your ad reach, frequency, conversions, and costs.

Using this data, you can analyze and make changes to your campaign. For example, if you're not getting enough clicks, you can try an ad with different ad copy or graphics to see if it would get more clicks.

By looking at the data, you can see if your ad is getting enough impressions or too many, adjust the demographics and target, and make other changes to see the impact on your ad results.

Testing and modifying an ad can significantly impact the campaign results. You can see the results by running your ad using a smaller budget and then deciding to increase your advertising budget.

I recommend running any specific campaign for 2-3 weeks before analyzing the results and making any changes. A few weeks will give your ad enough time to have enough impressions and collect enough data to make the statistics meaningful.

<u>Insights</u>

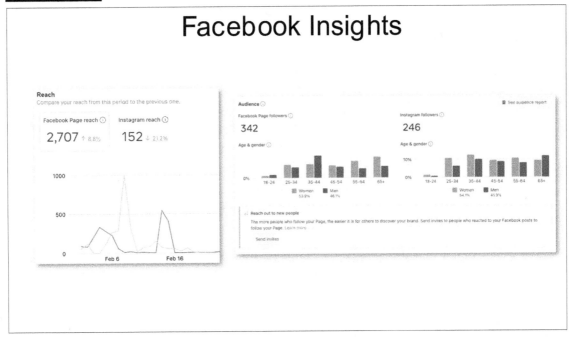

The Insights screen gives you feedback on your Page activity and post engagement, both organic and paid (ads). These statistics will help you understand what content your audience finds most appealing. Analyzing these figures and focusing on the kind of posts that have more engagement will improve your visibility. Data is provided in a table and graph format and for export to a spreadsheet.

When you open Insights, you see a lot of information. Let's take a look at what it means.

Insight Terms

You'll see charts that show the following:

- Actions on Page: number of clicks on a Facebook action you are using on your Page, such as your contact information or a call-to-action like a phone call.

- Page Views: the total number of views for your Page.

- Page Previews: people who hovered over your Page or profile picture to see a preview.

- Page Likes: the number of new Likes

- Reach: the number of people who saw your posts, organic and paid.

- Recommendations: number of times your Page was recommended.

- Post Engagements: the number of times people liked, commented, or shared your posts.

- Videos: the number of views your videos received.

- Followers: number of people who have followed your Page.

- Following a Page occurs when a user Likes it. Users have options when Following to change how they see your Posts:

  - Default: Facebook determines for the user how often Posts appear in their Newsfeed.

  - Unfollow: the user still Likes the Page but will never see Posts.

  - See First: Page posts appear at the top of the user's NewsFeed.

  - Notifications: set to "on" when a user Likes a Page but can be set to off. Events and Suggested Live Videos result in a Facebook notification email or message.

You'll be able to see information on how each one performs. The data tells you which posts are engaging and will help you direct your efforts to more of these types of content. The columns show this information:

- An icon for the kind of post (image, link, video, etc.)

- Targeting, which is almost always public for a Post.

- Reach by organic and paid.

- Engagement by type: Post Clicks, Reactions, Comments, and Shares.

- An opportunity to advertise the post with a Boost Post button.

Clicking on the Posts link in the left column displays insights on all Posts.

Other Insights Links

The other Insights links provide more detailed information and statistics. Here's a quick explanation of each one:

- Promotions: shows you statistics on any promotions or ads you're currently running

- Followers: total Page followers today and over time, unfollows, followers by organic and paid, where your Page follows happened (on your Page, website, etc.)

- Likes: a history of total Page Likes over time, number of unlikes, organic and paid Likes

- Reach: detailed daily information on the number of people who saw your post and Post Likes, Comments, and Shares. A reaction is a more elaborate form of a Like using the icons that appear when users tap the Like button. Reactions are emoticon symbols for a heart, thumbs up, and several other icons to provide a more detailed reaction other than a simple "Like."

- Page Views displays more detailed demographic information on who viewed your Page and the sources they came from (for example, a link on your website.)

- Page Previews: total previews and a breakdown by demographic.

- Actions: people who get directions, click to your website, click your phone, or click an Action button. For example, if you have an email signup button on your Page, the number of people that clicked it. Also includes demographic breakdowns.

- Posts: a list of all posts similar to the top 5 shown in the Overview but with information on when your posts are viewed and over what period.

- Events: people reached, Event page views, engagement, ticket purchases, and audience demographics.

- Videos: information on how often your videos were viewed and for how long. Videos viewed for more than three seconds and ten seconds are tracked to see if your videos are interesting once people start watching them. Statistics are provided for both video posts and promoted videos.

- People: aggregated data of the people who Like or Follow your Page by age, gender, and location, with country, city, and language information.

- Shop: total Shop views, purchases, and sales by day, week, month, quarter, and product.

- Messages: the number of conversations with people who messaged your Page if you use the Message button.

Reviewing this information helps evaluate which posts generate the most interest and what types of posts create the most significant engagement and, thus, the greatest exposure for your Page.

Facebook Blueprint

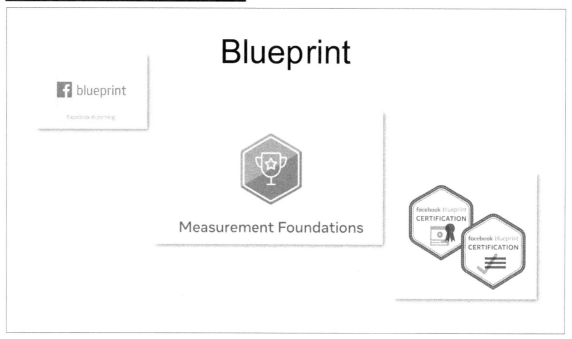

Facebook Blueprint is a free training and certification program available to anyone who wants to learn more about marketing using advertising on Facebook and Instagram. Facebook Blueprint has three parts: an online education program, a certification program, and an instructor-led classroom program called Facebook Blueprint Live. Let's review each of these so you can see whether they are helpful for you.

You need a Facebook Page to use Facebook Blueprint since most courses are designed to help you understand how to promote a brand and use advertising. After registering for Facebook Blueprint, you can access the eLearning, Certification, and Live links and start taking courses.

Facebook Blueprint eLearning

Facebook offers an extensive online learning catalog of courses for all levels of marketers and all sizes of businesses, with courses designed for Facebook and Instagram, which is owned by Facebook. Most courses are 15 minutes in length and include a short "knowledge check" exam if you want to review what you learned and prepare for certification.

All courses are self-paced, so you can start any class, and your account will track your completed courses and progress.

Courses are organized by topics and labeled for beginners or advanced learners so you can select the appropriate course for your current skill level.

Topics include:

- Ad Placements and Formats
- Advanced Best Practices
- Advertising Objectives
- Best Practices to Get Started
- Building Your Presence on Facebook and Instagram
- Campaign Optimization
- Creative
- Instagram
- Introduction to Facebook Apps and Services
- Measurement and Reporting
- Messenger
- Publisher Tools
- Purchasing and Managing Your Ads
- Small/Medium Business
- Solution-Based Ad Products
- Targeting

Use this link to view the courses: https://www.facebook.com/blueprint/courses

Learning Path

The above list of topics includes many courses for each, so the learning path option may help you find a set of classes tailored to your marketing role or the type of expertise you have using advertising on Facebook or Instagram.

You can find them at this link https://www.facebook.com/business/learn/paths

- All Content Analyst
- Brand Marketer
- Growing Your Business on Facebook (Getting Started)
- Growing Your Business on Facebook (Advanced)
- C-Suite Executive
- Creative and Strategic Planner
- Data Driven Marketer
- Digital Buyer
- Direct Response

66

- Reporting and Analytics
- Gaming Publisher
- TV Buyer

The Growing Your Business on Facebook (Getting Started) path is an excellent example since it fits most students who take my classes. This path includes courses to help you understand the basics of advertising on Facebook and Instagram, including courses on ad policies, how to create different types of ads using the Ads Manager, how a campaign works, creating a Facebook Page, understanding how to manage your Facebook Page, using Instagram for your business, how you're charged for ads, targeting core audiences and some tools for creating videos and video ads.

Selecting a path enrolls you in all the courses in the learning path. It shows if you should take the courses in any particular order.

Certification and Exams

A Facebook certification can help you demonstrate a higher skill level for jobs as a digital marketing professional or help you identify qualified professionals with the expertise to help you with your marketing. Industry certifications are standard in high-tech and show that the individual who has one demonstrated some degree of knowledge on a topic using a consistent measurement like an exam.

Two certifications are available, the Facebook Certified Planning Professional and the Facebook Certified Buying Professional. Each certification requires taking the Core Competencies exam first as a pre-requisite.

The certification process requires that you pass two online or onsite (your choice) proctored exams with a passing score of 700. To take the online test, you'll need a computer with a webcam and microphone, and you'll have to show a valid form of identification, like a driver's license. You can schedule an exam at any time through your blueprint account, and the learning courses aren't a requirement for certification. A practice exam is available to see how well you'd score, and you should try it if you plan on working toward certification. Each exam costs about $150; a recertification test is required annually.

The Facebook Advertising Core Competencies exam measures skills in advertising policies and practices to manage Facebook Pages and to create, purchase and manage Facebook ads. It also measures your knowledge of advertising objectives and understanding of different roles in media planning and ad buying.

The Facebook Certified Buying Professional exam and certification are designed for people who focus on purchasing and placing ads on Facebook and Instagram. The process of buying, setting, and managing ad performance with so many different ad types is a valuable certification for anyone responsible for creating and purchasing ads.

The Facebook Certified Planning Professional team and certification focuses not so much on the ad buying process as the ad planning process and how to plan, execute, and measure results from an ad campaign.

You can pursue both certifications if you want or just one, depending on what would be of great value to you. Since the Core Competencies is a requirement for either certification, there's a substantial amount of subject matter expertise someone with either certification will have about Facebook and Instagram advertising.

The level of knowledge for certification assumes that you've worked as a professional in digital advertising for six months using Facebook and Instagram. Work experience isn't required, however. You can prepare for the exam by taking free online courses, but if you're just starting, taking all the courses necessary could take several weeks of full-time studying.

Try taking the practice exam to see how prepared you are to test your skill level. There's no charge; you can see what questions you answered incorrectly to focus on courses in those areas.

Pros and Cons

Facebook's blueprint program offers an extensive free online learning resource for advertisers, agencies, and professionals to study and learn about virtually any topic related to advertising on Facebook and Instagram. Blueprint focuses on advertising, not how to create and publish your content.

For a small business or entrepreneur, there are as many courses as you want, all available for free. From managing your Facebook Page to more advanced topics, you can learn as much as you want or need.

For a professional in digital marketing, the certification path can make a difference in getting a job, getting higher pay, or obtaining clients.

Website Links:

- https://www.facebook.com/blueprint/courses
- https://www.facebook.com/blueprint/courses/path
- https://www.facebook.com/business/learn/certification

WHY BLOG

I believe a Blog makes the best website for almost anyone or any organization. Blogs offer a few things other websites don't include or make easy to accomplish. It's not just my opinion. Every online marketing agency recommends a website with a blog function as the best type of website for online marketing.

Easy publishing

Blogs make adding and editing content easy with WYSIWYG (what you see is what you get) writing and publishing tools. You can quickly create new content and change existing content on your website.

SEO

Blogs make search engines happy. Every headline is in an HTML (HyperText Markup Language) format that search engines always search for (the H1 tag format). Blogs, being all about content, have lots of text for search engines to index, and blogs are updated much more frequently than websites, which results in higher SEO rankings. A blog keeps the content in chronological order (and by topic or category), whereas a website without a blog does not. Every post creates a new page on the website, adding to the total content on the site.

Easy to manage settings and design

Blog sites are easy to manage by people with no programming or web design experience. All blogs allow you to sell advertising and manage your design, layout, and other settings.

Blogs allow you to create and update content from mobile devices. The easier it is to update your website from any location, the more frequently you'll likely do it.

My recommendation for the new blogger is to use Google's blogging service, Blogger, which is easy to learn and use. You can start one at www.blogger.com.

Comments

Comments allow bloggers (people who write or publish blogs) to build a community for their blogs. The ability to post an article or post, and get written feedback from readers, is similar to an editor writing a newspaper editorial and publishing letters to the editor. With the web, this feedback process takes place in minutes or less.

Mobile

Blogs work well on mobile devices. Good website designers ensure that a website will be displayed on any computer, web browser, and mobile device. Recent industry studies reveal that more than 50% of all website visits come from mobile devices, and it's increasing. Google evaluates websites to determine if it's "mobile-friendly" and ranks sites that format for smartphones higher in search results on smartphones. Desktop and laptop views of websites have smaller text links that, while easy to click on with a mouse, are more challenging for a finger to tap. A mobile-friendly website version reformats the layout when viewed on a smartphone or other small-screen device so a visitor can use their finger to navigate the site using smartphone-friendly icons and buttons.

RSS

Using RSS allows a blog author to distribute his content to his subscribers. Suppose someone is an authority or has an interesting blog. In that case, readers can receive updates from the RSS feed process almost immediately. Almost all blogging sites and software have standard RSS capability.

Many blogs include options and tools to send blog posts directly to social networks. Social networks can receive RSS posts and repost them on social network sites. If your blog doesn't have a tool to link to a specific social network, third-party services like Hootsuite, Buffer, dlvr.it, and IFTTT offer ways to broadcast your blog posts to your social network accounts.

Auto-posting with Social

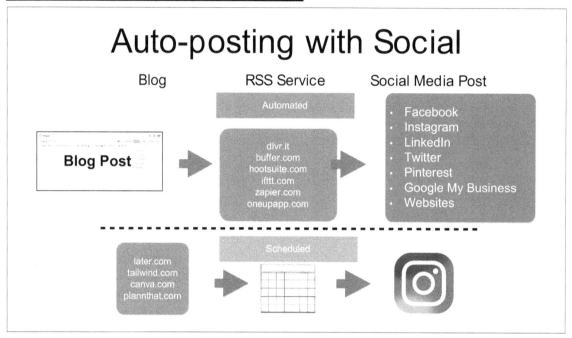

RSS, which stands for Real Simple Syndication, is a technology used on the web, primarily on blogs, to broadcast a blog's updates to the internet. For people who subscribe to an RSS feed, using an RSS "reader" software will provide them with updates from the blog or website when new content is posted or updated.

Social Media Posting

Because most social media sites use RSS for posts and status updates, Blogs have become the choice for anyone trying to publicize anything since all blogs come with RSS feeds. Many blog add-ons allow you to automatically publish the headlines from your blog to your Facebook, Twitter, LinkedIn, and other accounts. Check with your website service to see if they have a built-in tool for auto-posting.

Many site owners post more frequently on their social media accounts. Using their RSS feed, they can display updates to their website or even from one social media account to another.

Automating Blog Posts to Social Networks

Setting up an account with social networking automation sites is usually free for a few social media accounts. When you want to connect to more social networks, you'll have to upgrade to a paid version, starting at about $20 monthly.

You can push content from your blog to your social networking accounts using these tools:

- dlvr.it
- buffer.com
- hootsuite.com
- ifttt.com
- zapier.com
- Oneupapp.com
- Later.com
- Tailwind.com
- Canva.com
- Plannthat.com

Each of these sites has helpful information on finding your blog's RSS feed and setting up the connection to your social accounts. In addition to distributing your blog posts, most of these services offer the ability to post and schedule directly from their website.

Instagram Scheduling

If you connect your Facebook Page to your Instagram account. In that case, Meta offers the Meta Business page where you can manage and schedule your posts for both Instagram and Facebook. However, you can't use it for any other social network.

Some services listed above have built connections to Instagram to allow you to auto-post from your blog. However, most tools mentioned above have a website to schedule your posts. These services include a web dashboard with a calendar to prepare your images and text for posting. Some of the auto-posting RSS services include an Instagram calendar as a feature.

Remember that Instagram doesn't always allow your posts to include links to webpages until you reach a minimum number of followers, currently 10,000, so it's not as good at driving traffic to your website as other social networks.

What problem does RSS solve?

RSS allows people to see what's updated on a website without subscribing to emails and having a flooded inbox. The headlines of the latest articles are visible when the reader looks at their RSS reader software or mobile app. It solves the problem of keeping up-to-date without the need to receive emails.

The RSS feed does not contain all the new content, usually just a headline or a snippet of information to help the reader determine if he wants to read more. If so, then clicking on the link for the article takes him to the blog or web page where the full article appears.

One way to keep updated with new articles published on a website is to subscribe to an email list that sends you a message anytime something new is posted. Subscribing to updates this way might be OK if you visited one or two websites or blogs and they only published something new once a week. You wouldn't have more than a few emails from the websites coming in each week, and it would be manageable. But what if you wanted to keep up with new articles from a few dozen or more sites? RSS helps you keep up to date without the need for emails.

Instead of signing up for an email update, subscribe to the website's RSS feed. To do this, look for a "subscribe" link or an RSS Feed icon and click on it.

When you "subscribe" to the RSS feed, you don't get emails sent to you every time there is an update from the site. What will appear is a list of articles from all of the websites you subscribe to when you use your RSS "reader." So let's look at what applications are available for subscribing to RSS feeds.

RSS reader software and Twitter

At one time, the only way to subscribe to RSS was to use a separate application called an RSS Reader. Some web browsers and email services support RSS. Twitter offers a simple and easy-to-use solution for subscribing to blogs since most bloggers auto-post their articles on their Twitter accounts.

Where do you get a Blog

For the beginner, I recommend learning with Google's website, Blogger. It's easy to get started, free, and simple to use. Setting up a Blogger account takes only three simple steps.

Go to Blogger.com. If you have a Google account, you can use it to start your blog; if you don't, Blogger will ask you to set one up. All you will need is an email address (and it doesn't need to be Gmail).

The next step is to choose a name for your blog, which can be anything you want. You can change it anytime, so don't worry about picking one you might not like later. Blog sites need a unique URL, and with Blogger, you will start out using Blogger's URL with your name in it. You cannot use a URL name that someone else has already used. Since Blogger hosts the blog, all URLs are in the format www.yourname.blogspot.com. You now have a web address, which you use to direct people to your blog. The last step is to pick a design template.

Other popular websites that are also blogs include WordPress, Wix, Weebly, TypePad, Squarespace, GoDaddy, and Shopify.

OTHER SOCIAL NETWORKS

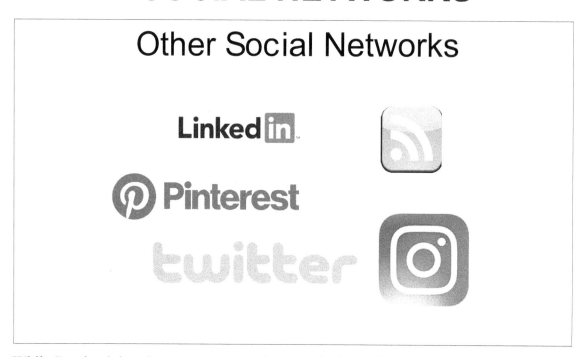

While Facebook has the most users, another may be better for your marketing efforts. If you want to explain how to use your product or how you perform your service, a video on YouTube is excellent. If you have expertise or knowledge you want to share, Twitter is a good choice. Suppose you can deliver your content and message with images. In that case, Instagram will work. If you have physical products, designs, or recipes, Pinterest is where people search for ideas. These are just some reasons to use one of the other widely used social networks.

Your priority should always be to choose a network that reaches your target audience. Focus on one social network, either organically or with paid advertising. Organic marketing means committing to deliver valuable posts on your account on a scheduled basis to give the users content they can consume. Paid advertising options are available on all social networking sites. They can help you reach your targeted audience with or without organic content.

Each has its strengths and weaknesses and often has different users. Keeping up with all the social media sites can be challenging for a small business, so start by choosing the best one for your goals and objectives. The right network(s) will be the one that allows you to reach your target audience most effectively.

Most of the principles of using Facebook apply to other sites, so you don't have to start learning social media marketing from scratch. Posting updates and providing valuable and engaging content are principles that work on all sites.

Virtually everything we learned about how to use Facebook applies to other social networks for marketing. An organic approach uses your content to build and leverage an audience, while paid advertising can increase your reach and results to accelerate your results.

Being a proficient social network user will help you be a better marketer on that service. I recommend you learn to use social networks and become familiar with how people use them before starting marketing.

To help you prioritize, I've created guidelines that follow the most popular ones. These include Twitter, LinkedIn, Instagram, Pinterest, and YouTube. The following information will help you decide which site or sites best suit your goals.

Followers and Following

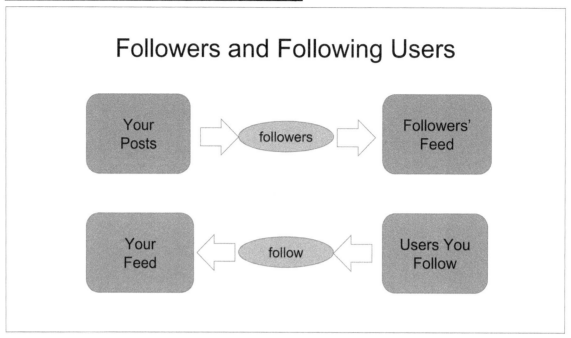

Instagram, Twitter, LinkedIn, Pinterest, and Facebook use a concept called "following." Users click on a "follow" button and opt-in to see the posts from that account in their feed. People follow other people, businesses, non-profits, and any other account, so it's easier to see updates from those accounts. A user's account information includes links to any account they follow, so it's easier to find posts. In this way, following serves a function similar to a bookmark or favorite in a web browser.

For anyone to see your posts, they can search for you, or they can subscribe to you by becoming a follower. Some users will follow you if you follow them, but there's no established etiquette. Anytime a user starts following you, the social network notifies you (email or status update), letting you know you have a new follower. You don't have to approve it, but you can block them from following you if you don't want them to see your tweets. By going to the user's profile, you may decide to follow them if you think their tweets will be helpful. The reverse happens for you when you follow a user; they may choose to follow you if they find your tweets worthwhile.

Building followers is critical to visibility on social networks; frequently posting helpful content is essential to build followers. Most experts on social media recommend a daily post to attract and develop a following but use a schedule that you can manage, and don't let your content quality suffer just for quantity.

If building a following is proving difficult, try changing the content in your posts. Doing your competitive research and following what other businesses or organizations similar to you post will help you see what is appealing to the audience you're trying to reach.

Instagram

Instagram

- Photo sharing
- 1 Billion+ monthly active users
- 89% of users outside U.S.
- 50% users 18-29 Y.O.
- About 50/50 male/female
- 25 Million+ businesses on Instagram
- Discovery, fashion brands, design, style, products, quality photos, influencers
- Can manage Facebook and Instagram from Meta

https://business.instagram.com/advertising/

Instagram is an online social networking service that allows users to take photos and videos, apply filters and other effects, and share them. It's a free service and a fun way to share photos and videos. It's also owned by Meta and includes a feature allowing Instagram users to post to their Facebook accounts.

Unlike Facebook, Instagram users don't have friends. Users follow other users to receive their posts in the feed, but virtually all posts on Instagram are public. Instagram is a social network that helps people discover new things.

Users of Instagram use the Instagram app on their smartphones. The user takes a picture or video of their desired subject matter, then uses one of the filters available on Instagram to change the image, and then shares the photo or video on Instagram.

The filters give any picture a "professional" look with the touch of a button. While it doesn't replace a professional photographer, Instagram helps make photos look better, making it useful for most people.

What the filters do.

There are many filters and effects available on Instagram. But I'll mention some of the more popular ones.

Each filter has an optional border and changes the photo's look by enhancing the colors or creating soft glows or vintage looks. Instagram effects are not limited to digital filters.

The tilt-shift feature allows the user to apply an adjustable bar or circular focus on the photo, creating the appearance of an altered depth of field. Effects can make images that resemble what photographers take with specialty lenses, turning a standard cell phone picture into an artistic and professional-looking photograph.

A rotate button can rotate a photo clockwise 90 degrees each time it's tapped, allowing users to change the orientation of their image as needed.

Captions, labels, and tags

Users can also add information to explain the photo, include a search term, and identify themselves or other Instagram users. Text, including hashtags, can be added below each image. The hashtag allows other users to find and search for photos.

Using an @ symbol before a person's username creates a "tag" to identify the user's account in the post. Tagged images include a link to the user account so viewers can click to see that user's account.

Once the user is finished applying filters and effects to their photograph, it is automatically shared online with Instagram. The photos can be printed at photo centers and appear in a 4"x4" square reminiscent of Polaroid photos.

History and use of Instagram

Launched in October of 2010 by Kevin Systrom and Mike Krieger, Instagram had over 10 million users and over 150 million photo uploads in less than a year. Acquired by Facebook in 2012, Instagram now has hundreds of millions of active users and is still growing. It's one of the most popular social networks in the under-24 age range.

Marketing on Instagram

Instagram Marketing

Organic

- Instagram posts - image or video from smartphone

- Use multiple hashtags on topics

- Focus on followers

- No links to websites in posts

- High-quality images a must

Ads

- Must use Facebook Business Page
- No Instagram account required
- Brand awareness
- Reach
- Traffic
- Engagement
- Video views
- Lead generation
- Messages
- Conversions
- Product sales
- Store visits

Instagram is a community of people who like to see quality photographs. If your business or brand has a good source of photo material you can shoot with your smartphone, Instagram is an important social network. Certain types of people are more active users, such as photographers and photojournalists. Still, anyone with a smartphone and a good eye for a good picture is likely a user.

Some professions have a high concentration of users. These include publishing, fashion, design, performers, architects, and the travel and tourist industry. High-quality photos and videos are essential to building an Instagram following

Organic

Some helpful tips for using Instagram are:

- Become familiar with your smartphone's app, filters, and other features.

- Hashtags are used on Instagram and will help people find your content, so include a hashtag appropriate to your content and always add a word or two about your photo as a caption explaining it. You can use several hashtags in a single post, so don't be afraid to use a few.

- Focus on posting regularly to build up a following. Follow other users and connect your Facebook account.

- You can't link to websites in a post, so your focus is building followers.

- Practice using your smartphone camera and editing photos. You can post using your camera or images form your library.

Advertising on Instagram requires that you use your Facebook Page. Facebook, which owns Instagram, recommends letting ads appear across both Facebook and Instagram networks. The process of creating, targeting, and running an ad is the same on Instagram and Facebook.

Ads

You can run ads on Instagram to achieve the same goals as on Facebook:

- Brand awareness
- Reach
- Traffic
- Engagement
- Video views
- Lead generation
- Messages
- Conversions
- Product sales
- Store visits

You can learn more about Instagram advertising at this link:

https://business.instagram.com/advertising/

Twitter

Twitter

- Over 300 Million users
- 24% of online adults use it
- 42% of users access daily
- 22.5% users - 25-34 Y.O.
- Journalists, entertainment, sports, subject-matter experts, brand names
- Local targeting

Get out there with Twitter Ads and be what's happening.

https://business.twitter.com/solutions

Twitter calls itself a "rudimentary" social networking service. It has gained popularity because it is relatively simple to use and restricts the length of a message. It was designed from the start to use mobile text and SMS messaging services available on cellular phones, the web, and email. In the United States, our cell phone carriers (Verizon, ATT, etc.) have text messaging services, also known as SMS, for Short Messaging Services.

Before 2017, Twitter had a limit of 140 characters in a post, also called a tweet. The length was due to text messaging services limiting the message to 160 characters; Twitter used 20 characters for the user address in their account, so 140 characters remained for the message content. As smartphones and the Twitter mobile app became how most people used Twitter, the company expanded the message limit to 280 characters.

With so many tweets, users may not see your post when they aren't using Twitter. You can safely repost the same tweet a second time to catch people during different times of the day. Marketing studies have shown that the second time a tweet appears, it obtains more than 65% of the engagement of the first post.

Twitter has stopped allowing third-party services to set up automated reposting of tweets. But you can schedule your post manually.

Twitter Terms

Unlike Facebook, which has Pages, Twitter has accounts. All accounts are used the same, whether for a person or business and using more than one account is possible. All you need is a different email for each account.

Users can retweet a tweet, which sends a tweet to their followers. Users with large followings can communicate and forward information to a broad audience. When someone retweets one of your tweets, they send it to all their followers.

Twitter is like a giant electronic telephone tree when communicating information. If I call two people, who call two people, who call two people, pretty soon, many people will know about something. Messages can spread very fast and efficiently. Twitter is like a telephone tree but uses the internet and multiple followers to enable rapid broadcasting.

Tweets

Twitter messages don't stay in front of people for a long time, though, and being visible on Twitter requires a commitment to regular posting. One post a day is necessary to increase your followers. With that commitment can come great rewards, though, since many people in media, press, and other fields follow users on Twitter to keep up on the latest news and information.

URL Shorteners

Although the 280-character message may initially seem limited, Twitter users have become creative when using a URL in a post to direct you to a website. Since each URL character takes up space, URL shorteners create a URL with fewer characters. Tools such as www.goo.gl (Google), www.bit.ly, and www.tinyurl.com shorten a URL to a few characters and allow Twitter users to send links to websites, including their website, blog, and landing pages. Using a URL shortener creates more space for other text in the body of the tweet.

Some websites have tools that repost social media content, including URL shorteners. The add-on creates a shortened link, along with the blog post's title.

In addition to URL shortening tools, if your website is a blog with RSS capability, it can be connected to Twitter and other social media sites using RSS connection services. These connection services automatically create a short URL to link your post to your site.

Hashtags

What some people know as the pound symbol "#" is also called a hashtag. When the pound symbol appears before a word or phrase in a tweet, it's called a hashtag. There are no spaces between the hashtag and the phrase, so it appears as "#smallbiz" in a tweet (without the quotes).

Hashtags are a topic index because every hashtag is a link that will cause a user's account to display all tweets that include the hashtag. Because they create a clickable link, hashtags are used to organize and categorize tweets.

Here's how this works on Twitter. The pound sign symbol tells Twitter that the phrase is a hashtag. Twitter finds all the tweets using that hashtag phrase, then Twitter makes the tweets that include that hashtag into links that connect to each other. Clicking on a hashtag link in a tweet results in your screen showing only those tweets that contain the hashtag. Tweets are displayed chronologically, with the most recent tweet at the top of your list. The way Twitter displays the tweets makes it easier for users to find the most recent tweets about specific topics and to hold conversations.

Marketers can increase their visibility on Twitter by including the appropriate hashtag in the body of their tweets and increase the likelihood they will be found by users interested in that topic.

Community Conversations

Click on a hashtag that appears in a tweet, and your screen displays all the tweets that contain the hashtag. Unlike your Home page, which displays tweets from the users you follow, you're now following a hashtag topic on Twitter and only see tweets that contain that hashtag. This feature is valuable because of something that Twitter does for you automatically.

With the hashtag topic open in your display, when you post a tweet on your own, Twitter automatically inserts the hashtag in your tweet, so anyone following the hashtag will see your tweet in their display.

You can find tweets about a specific topic by clicking on a hashtag or using it to search Twitter.

Searching for Hashtags

Twitter has a search function that searches all tweets on Twitter, and you can use searching to help find hashtags even if you don't know one already. The magnifying glass icon opens the search screen; then, you enter a topic, person, word, or phrase. The search results show user accounts and tweets containing the search term. If the text you searched for is used in a hashtag, you'll see it in one of the tweets that appear in your search results.

People like to follow tweets about the games during a major live event such as an election, the World Series, or the Olympics. By searching for a term, for example, Olympics, you'll see the hashtags #olympics and #olympics2018. Each of these is a link on Twitter, so clicking one of them will display all of the tweets that include the hashtag. You can keep up to date or join the conversation with any user that included the hashtag in their tweet by adding it to yours

Using search or hashtags makes Twitter a great way to keep up-to-date on any live event or activity. You can find others posting updates about any topic, even if you're not connected to them as a follower on Twitter. If a hashtag is popular, Twitter features it in its "trending" topics list on everyone's Home page.

Hashtags on other Social Networks

While other social networks support hashtags, Twitter and Instagram are the two that have the most active usage. Hashtags only work within the social network. For example, a hashtag on Twitter will only link to content on Twitter, and hashtags on Instagram will only connect to the content on Instagram, but the topics are similar.

Creating Hashtags and Hashtag Etiquette

Anyone can create a hashtag using the pound symbol before a word or phrase. However, there are many common ones already in use on Twitter. The website www.hashtags.org includes a list of commonly used hashtags and a feature to search for hashtags.

Twitter offers a help page on creating hashtags with recommendations for how to use them at this link **http://support.twitter.com/articles/49309-using-hashtags-on-twitter.**

Using a hashtag to attract attention when the tweet isn't about the topic may result in a spam report. As a result, Twitter recommends only using a hashtag if the tweet is related to the subject and using at most two hashtags per tweet.

Marketing on Twitter

Twitter Marketing

Organic	Ads
• Twitter posts - article, video, image (accepts RSS feeds) • Use hashtags on topics • Follow journalists and media • Use local place names • Promotions and limited-time offers	• Visibility • Promoted posts • Tweet engagements • Followers • Website links • Search ads

Organic

If you're promoting your expertise or have timely promotions, Twitter is a network to consider for your marketing. For a business with specials or promotions, letting prospects and customers know if they follow you, they will get updates is a helpful approach. Mobile food carts use Twitter to announce their location, estimated time of arrival, and daily specials to their customers. Large brands use Twitter to promote sales and special events with an expiration date or limited quantity. Users who watch for these types of activity set their notifications for alerts.

A user can set up notifications from Twitter by the account they follow. Instead of just seeing tweets in their feed, users can change settings so they are notified by text or email when an account they follow posts a tweet. Users who want to be the first to know about something use this feature to keep up-to-date and to find valuable promotions they can forward to their followers.

Twitter is very popular with the media industry and can be used as a form of public relations. Journalists are all active users on Twitter and use it to find subject matter experts, breaking stories and ideas for their print, radio, or television broadcasts. Follow some journalists or industry experts in your field; if you have good content, you'll see growth in followers.

Other industries are very active on Twitter, including technology, sports, entertainment, and publishing. To determine if Twitter is the right social media platform for you, see if your customers or potential customers use it or if your professional contacts use it. If not, remember that almost every journalist uses Twitter, so your stories can be picked up as news if they are appealing. Twitter makes an excellent public relations social media network.

For marketing purposes, Twitter is useful for communicating information as you build up followers and can be an excellent form of public relations and media awareness. Remember, it's a matter of who you are trying to reach and if your potential audience and target include Twitter users. Twitter should be part of your social media marketing plan if it does.

Ads

Twitter has advertising programs for large brands and small/local businesses. One program promotes your account to increase followers, and another promotes tweets to increase exposure and sharing of your messages. An additional advertisement will drive traffic to your website. Signing up and targeting an audience locally and by audience interests is possible.

Setting up ads and targeting users by their interests and demographics is similar to Facebook but simpler. Twitter learns about its users based on their profile, location, the tweets they view, the users they follow, and their engagement on Twitter with comments and shares. Based on this tracking, Twitter has excellent audience targeting based on users' interests.

To start advertising on Twitter, you need to change your account to a business account, which is free. Once you make the change, you can create ads and monitor your ad statistics.

You can learn more about advertising on Twitter at this link:

https://business.twitter.com/solutions

LinkedIn

LinkedIn

- B2B social network
- Over 1 Billion users
- 50/50 male/female demographics
- 51% of college graduates use it
- 90 million senior level influencers
- 10 million C-level executives

https://business.linkedin.com/marketing-solutions

LinkedIn is a professional business-to-business social network. It started as a service for business professionals in the workplace to keep up with their contacts and to encourage career development by posting a resume-type profile. With a database of resumes, LinkedIn could sell access to the database to recruiters, marketers, and employers. Suppose your targeted audience consists of workplace professionals. In that case, LinkedIn is a social network that you should include in your marketing effort.

Personal and Company Profiles

LinkedIn has both personal and Company profiles. Users create a profile by filling out forms on LinkedIn. Anyone who works at a company can create a Company page by completing a series of forms. Company profiles include information on products and services. All of this is free.

Most users on LinkedIn form relationships with business contacts. These direct connections enable a user to message anyone in his contact list. It's possible to search for people on LinkedIn. Until a user connects with another user, he can't send a direct message unless he upgrades to a paid account. Similar to how a connection with friends on Facebook requires that both parties agree to it, a connection on LinkedIn requires a user to accept an invite.

If a user wants to communicate with someone they're not connected to, a paid account allows them to send a message. LinkedIn charges a monthly fee based on the number of messages. The premium service is helpful for sales, marketing, consulting, and recruiters who want to reach people they're not connected to already.

Recommendations

LinkedIn is a way to develop a reputation for a professional and a business using the Recommendations feature. A recommendation is a message by one Linked user about another LinkedIn user. Recommendations are listed on a user and corporate profile and are a form of testimonial. Users can send a recommendation request to any of their connections, which is how most users obtain their recommendations. A user can also write one for a business if that business has a company listing on LinkedIn. Since LinkedIn is a site focused on professional networking, recommendations are valuable for any user to evaluate a prospective employee, consultant, or company when considering their products or services.

Groups

Groups are an active activity on LinkedIn. Groups enable users to connect with others in their expertise, learn about professional topics, and create exposure for themselves. Groups are free to join, and the Group administrator manages the membership. Many options are available, from very private to public and open. Within groups, most activity is discussions. Any member can start a conversation, pose a question, and reply to one.

Active group members use their discussion activities to demonstrate subject matter expertise and establish a reputation. Group membership is also a way to develop new connections since Group membership is a way to reach out to another individual and request a connection. More experienced users often establish their Group to attract an audience. When creating a Group, the user becomes the Group Administrator and can send periodic messages to the entire group, promote a discussion topic, and moderate the Group activity.

Status Updates on LinkedIn

LinkedIn has a Status Update option for posting information. Status updates are broadcast to all connections through daily or weekly email announcements, depending on the user's preferences. Third-party applications allow reposting to Twitter, importing a blog, and importing slides from SlideShare, a widely used service owned by LinkedIn for sharing PowerPoint presentations.

LinkedIn is very much a business-to-business networking site. Using LinkedIn is probably unnecessary if your products or services are focused on consumers. LinkedIn should be a priority for your marketing plan if your target customer includes the corporate market and people with job titles in company positions. Join groups and make sure you have as complete a personal or corporate profile as possible, then start building connections from your existing contacts and group memberships. Participating in discussions will increase your visibility significantly on LinkedIn.

Marketing on LinkedIn

LinkedIn Marketing

Organic

- LinkedIn posts - article, video, image (accepts RSS feeds)

- Company Page - free

- Group participation

- Group ownership - manage members and send an email to members

- Premium account for InMail

Ads

- Sponsored content

- Promoted posts

- Followers

- Engagement

- Website visits

- Lead generation

- Impressions

- Video Views

- Jobs

Organic

Many users of LinkedIn create a profile, essentially a resume, and then aren't sure what to do with LinkedIn. Active users use LinkedIn to search and communicate with other professionals, using the service as an online resource for professional networking. If you think of LinkedIn as a networking tool, your activity and engagement with other users will increase.

Connections and Posts
One way to start is by connecting with other people you know. Use the search field to locate other professionals you already know. Once connected with them, you can send direct messages through LinkedIn. Like any other business networking practice, trying to make a sales or marketing approach as a first contact can limit your response. Commenting on another professional's posts and posting your own content that showcases your skills, expertise, and knowledge are the most effective types of content on LinkedIn.

Groups
To really increase your engagement, join or start a group. Joining a group of professionals with a common interest will connect you with other users. Some groups are public, others are private and require permission to join, but all are beneficial. Search for groups related to your profession or expertise. Once in the group, you should participate. You can ask a question, introduce yourself, or add content. Your business or organization's promotion depends on the group's policies, so visit the group to see what kind of content is added and discussed. Group members that are active contributors are featured on the group's page, creating visibility.

For the most impact, start your own group. Like Facebook, groups are free to create. The key to creating your own group is to start seeding it with content that will attract people, so you'll have to start posting to get it launched. However, from my experience with several groups I've started, the members keep adding content to their visibility once you get others to join.

As a group owner, you can feature a post at the top of the group and send an announcement email to all the members. But use the announcement feature sparingly since some members may turn off group notifications if they are too frequent.

Ads

Since any aspect of a user profile is searchable, targeting a user audience by job title, location, or other information is possible. Any user, personal or corporate, can create and purchase LinkedIn advertising. Like advertising on other social networks, the ads appear to a user when viewing LinkedIn. Pay-per-click and impression ads are available, and the process for setting up a campaign is similar to Facebook's.

One of the most effective ads on LinkedIn is for lead generation since LinkedIn is a social network of professionals, a high percentage of whom are decision-makers.

Advertising can promote a post and increase followers and clicks to a website.

Other ad types include impressions, video views, and a separate job category.

You can learn more about LinkedIn advertising at this link:

https://business.linkedin.com/marketing-solutions

Pinterest

Pinterest

- Over 500 Million users
- 70% women, 16% male
- 70% have a college degree
- 60% children 5 or under
- 34% of users earn $50K-$75K/yr
- Visuals by users and brands
- Over 50% of users make a purchase of a promoted pin
- Inspiration, ideas, DIY, products, food, home, fashion, travel, etc.
- 60% of pins are brands and products

https://business.pinterest.com/en/our-audience
https://business.pinterest.com

Pinterest has become one of the top ten websites used on the internet. Pinterest is a free service that allows users to "pin" any photo on the internet to one of their "boards." Users create their accounts with several categories of boards, which are very much like a traditional bulletin board, and all boards are public and shareable between users. Find a photo on the Web, and with a few clicks, you can pin it to one of your boards.

There's not much profile information, so privacy isn't a significant concern for users, giving users a sense of freedom for posting and sharing. It's possible to follow any other user. Since all a user does is post photos from the Web, Pinterest has become a favorite way for people to share interests in a very graphical format. Copyright infringement of an image has been an issue, and some photo sites, including Flickr, don't allow Pinterest posting of copyrighted material. However, brands and marketers often include the Pinterest "pin" button on their website, encouraging visitors to Pin a photo to Pinterest.

Users like Pinterest because it's easy to use and allows sharing and following interests and other users. Brands use Pinterest because Pinterest users use the site for discovery and ideas. Pinterest suggests boards for home decor, weddings, style (fashion), and design. The suggestions for boards and activities are focused on products.

Pinterest makes money by linking any product image a user shares to an affiliate program, which pays a commission if someone purchases the product. In effect, Pinterest has created a community of window shoppers who make personal online catalogs for free. Savvy marketers use the links from any photos and images posted to link back to their web page or to an affiliate program that pays them for a purchase.

Marketing on Pinterest

Pinterest Marketing

Organic

- Pins - image (accepts RSS feeds)
- Create boards by category
- Post from blog or website so link is included
- Upload images and add link
- Add Pin button to your website

Ads

- Promoted posts
- Impressions
- Website clicks
- Engagement (closeup, repin, click on pin)
- Video impressions
- Buyable Pin - requires approval and shopping cart (Shopify, etc.)

Pinterest works best for physical items that can be displayed with a photo. While not as effective for services, some services that lend themselves to images, like food or travel, can be effective on Pinterest.

Pinterest has a devoted user base of hundreds of millions of users. The demographic is focused on women with families and discretionary income. A recent poll of users by Pinterest indicated that 60% of them say they are ready to buy a product when looking for it on Pinterest.

You can learn more about the Pinterest audience at this link:

https://business.pinterest.com/en/our-audience

Organic

When posting a photo on Pinterest, use the edit function to link back from the image to the website you want a user to see when they click the picture. Pinterest makes "pin it" buttons for websites to use as a marketing tool, which will encourage visitors to your site to "pin" your photos and images, and can generate more traffic to your site.

RSS feed services will connect your blog to Pinterest so you can auto-post. Be sure to create a board with the category for your pictures. With a business account (you can make any account a business account by using the link https://business.pinterest.com), you can obtain an HTML code to add the Pin button to your website. It's also possible to upload images from your computer but add a URL so people can click on the Pin.

Ads

Pinterest offers to advertise using the Promoted Pin feature. Promoted Pins enable you to choose a specific pin and add search terms. Pins are assigned to a topic when you post them, and the topics are searchable by users. When users search for a word or phrase, the Pin appears in search results, similar to a Google or Bing search. When people click on the Pin, they link to your Pinterest account or website.

There are several other ad options on Pinterest:

- Promoting a Pin by Impressions

- Promoting a Pin by website clicks

- Engagement - hover over your pin (closeup), RePin your Pin, Click on the Pin

- Video views

- Buyable Pin - a buyable pin requires a shopping cart that can supply Pinterest with a product for purchase and approval by Pinterest. You create your shopping cart in a service like Shopify, then submit your items for review to Pinterest. Once approved, you can purchase Buyable Pins, and people can order your product directly from Pinterest.

You can learn more at this link:

https://business.pinterest.com

YouTube and Video

The time spent watching online videos has been increasing yearly, and YouTube is still the top destination for video online. YouTube has its share of animal videos, but the use of brands and original content has increased to the point where almost every internet user has viewed a video on YouTube. It's widely used as a brand marketing site to explain products and services to prospects and to offer customer support through "how-to" videos.

YouTube makes it easy for anyone who can shoot a video with a camera or smartphone to publish videos. A user account on YouTube is free to create and upload videos. It's not only a web hosting location for videos. It's a channel that supports subscriptions. Subscribers with YouTube accounts who opt-in to a channel receive email updates when new videos are available. YouTube allows users to publish unlimited videos anytime, but you may have time limits on the length if you are a new user.

In addition to the channel feature of YouTube, YouTube supports feedback and ing through ratings and sharing functions. As a result, a video on YouTube can help any marketer reach a wider audience. YouTube videos appear in search results because Google owns YouTube.

Creating video

Publishing video on YouTube is relatively easy with today's tools for uploading videos from almost any source. Smartphone and tablet users can shoot and upload videos using the YouTube smartphone app. Portable camcorders and most still cameras all include the ability to make videos and transfer them to a computer.

Editing is possible with mobile editing tools like iMovie (free for iPhone, iPad, and Mac) and Google's Movie Studio for Android. Microsoft has a free editor called ClipChamp for Windows.

Producing long videos is unnecessary; people prefer videos that get the point across. Sound quality is essential, distinguishing between a good and a poorly made video. You will need an accessory microphone for whatever video recorder you use to record quality sound. Mics are available from online stores for iPhone, Android, and cameras. Most Single Lens Reflex cameras record video and have an audio jack for a microphone.

Advertising and SEO on YouTube

YouTube allows posting for free but controls the advertising on the site. Google sells advertising on YouTube with ads that appear in the video based on keyword tags and enables video publishers to make money with video advertising by accepting ads. You choose to allow ads or not; it's all controlled by you.

Owned by Google, YouTube is completely searchable by search engines, and YouTube results are often featured in Google's search results. When you post videos, use "tags" to describe the content and make your video searchable by search sites and users.

Video titles should include any keywords people use to find your content. It's also possible to use a transcription of the video for closed-caption, which Google can index for search results.

Social Video

Facebook, Twitter, Instagram, and Pinterest support video posting. However, be sure to use a visually self-explanatory video. You see many videos on social media with captions because people don't always have a headset or earbuds for playback.

If you think about it, it makes sense since most people are viewing social media on smartphones, and the sound of a video might be annoying to anyone nearby. If you use a video on social media, use action that tells a story. If you use annotations or text overlay, make sure it's big enough to be read.

SnapChat

Snapchat is a smartphone application that shares messages (called Snaps) between friends containing videos and photos with captions. The primary way of using Snapchat results in text, images, and videos being deleted automatically after viewing. The sender of an image or video decides how long the recipient can see the image, from one second to ten seconds.

Snapchat has fun and helpful image annotation tools that add special effects and allow users to make notes and draw on an image before sending it.

Snapchat, compared to other social networks

Created by a group of Stanford students who wanted to build a multimedia-sharing application that didn't save any of the shared content, the idea resulted in Snapchat. Other social networking sites like Facebook, Twitter, and LinkedIn keep a user's photos, videos, updates, and other shared content as part of the user's history of activity on the site.

As a result, all of a person's activity on a traditional social network becomes a historical journal. Snapchat's appeal is that anything that's shared is typically destroyed, and there is no personal history for anyone to view.

Like other social networking applications, users establish connections with an invitation. On SnapChat, invitations are sent using a cellular number. The invited user has to accept the invitation for two people to share anything with each other. Once two people connect, they can send and receive Snapchat videos, photos, and text messages with each other.

The combination of using a way to share with both parties agreeing to connect and the limited time that any shared content is available to view a more private and personal social network.

Snapchat has grown; it has added additional sharing options for its users where the content is not automatically deleted after viewing.

Other sharing options with Snapchat

Replay: The replay feature allows users to replay a previously deleted Snap. In any 24 hours, a user can only use Replay once.

Stories: Besides an individual video or photo message, sharing collections of images and videos with a group of friends is possible. Called a "Story," these messages can be viewed unlimited times for 24 hours before being automatically deleted.

Text: Users can text chat with other users, start a video chat if both parties are available simultaneously, and press a button that says "Here" to let the other know they want to chat.

Our Stories (meaning Stories created by Snapchat or partners)

Another way to use Snapchat allows users to follow activities while privacy settings allow public sharing. Events such as music concerts often have many Snapchat users in attendance. Snapchat uses the public Stories from all users and creates a Story from the user's shared content. A recent Star Wars convention in Anaheim was a Snapchat story. Viewers could see videos taken by Snapchat users who attended the event almost immediately after the videos were taken.

Snapchat has media partners that also create Stories about news and other content. These media outlets include CNN, National Geographic, and Cosmopolitan Magazine. Like a television channel, these providers add from three to ten stories to feature on Snapchat that are updated every 24 hours.

Marketing on Snapchat

SnapChat claims that they reach over 40% of all 18-34 year-olds in the United States, so it's the social network of choice for most of this demographic. If this is a target you want to reach, SnapChat may be helpful. Good quality content is required, just like any other social media site. People will connect with you and your brand based on the content, so your content can drive engagement, whether it's coupons and deals or product pictures.

Snaps can't be scheduled or posted from another source; you must use SnapChat to create a post. Any post can include a text message with your website URL, but it is not a link that people can click.

Businesses can place several ads that appear when a user views their feed. Here's a quick guide to the types of ads currently offered:

SnapAds are images or video ads that display in the user's feed when viewing Snaps. The video can be up to 10 seconds long and includes the option to swipe up to see more, which can be extended content such as a long video, article, app install ad, or a link to a mobile website.

Sponsored Geofilters are tiny piece of art that overlays a Snap and are applied by a user when taking a Snap near your location. It's useful for location-based marketing and is similar to the Facebook Check-In that announces a user's location. The geofilter message can be any message; the place triggers the option to apply it. This type of ad is excellent for businesses, organizations, and even individuals who want to promote themselves to nearby SnapChat users. Brand logos and trademarks are permitted.

Sponsored Lenses create a branded lens effect users can apply to their face in an image. Lenses are the features of SnapChat that add ears and noses to people's faces. A sponsored lens is a branded lens that includes a brand name. Sponsored lenses are commonly used by TV shows and movies to allow users to add a character's image to their face.

People such as performers willing to connect to others and publish in the My Stories type of Snap can connect with other users, who can then view the posts for up to 24 hours after they are posted.

You can learn more about using SnapChat for business at:

https://forbusiness.snapchat.com

PLANNING YOUR MARKETING

Now that you know some of what's involved in creating a Facebook Page and social media marketing, I recommend you begin a plan. While it may seem unnecessary, it helps to have something written down on paper that you can refer to when making decisions, communicating with others, and seeing how far you've come after starting. You can also revise the plan as you learn more and get feedback from your social media marketing efforts.

Before You Start

Before reviewing the steps to put together your social media marketing efforts, you should determine who will generate the content for posting. Your background and experience might have prepared you to run a business. Still, it may never have prepared you to be a writer, photographer, storyteller, or online advertiser, commonly called content creator.

Suppose your skills include the ability to create your own content. In that case, you have a tremendous advantage over other businesses, since you can create and personalize your content.

If these aren't your skills, or you don't want to spend the time creating content for posting, finding a resource or hiring someone to do this work will be necessary. Social media is about updates, and updates require fresh content.

If you have the skills, determine how much time and commitment you can make to do your social media marketing or hire someone to do it for you. Be honest in assessing your skills in creating content such as writing, photography, graphic design, video, and audio. Decide how much time you can set aside to learn how to use social media sites, set up your Page and other accounts, plan your advertising, and other activities such as deals, events, and responding to comments. Can you post content daily, weekly, or only once in a while?

Suppose you can't commit to an ongoing effort. In that case, you may consider contracting out some or all of your social media marketing. It's possible to contract for people to write posts, respond to comments, create accounts, update your status, and almost any social media aspect you may not want to do yourself. It's simply a matter of your budget.

Editorial Content Calendar

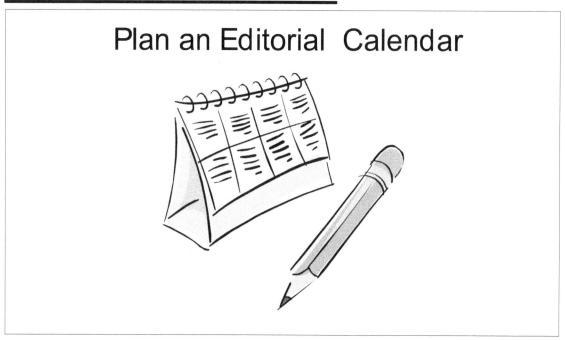

An editorial calendar is a schedule used to plan the publishing of content. Publications, from print magazines to online media, use their editorial calendar for planning. An example is a magazine planning for a summer issue and articles about family vacation ideas. Another example is a YouTube video channel that uses a calendar to schedule videos about product reviews.

An editorial calendar is a planning tool used by any media to schedule content. Blogs, websites, podcasts, newsletters, and social media accounts use an editorial calendar to plan and prepare episodes or articles. Using a calendar helps these publishers plan their work so they can start work on a specific piece of material far enough in advance, so it will be ready for publishing at the correct date and time.

Origin of the term

The term editorial calendar comes from an editor's role in producing any publication. The word content is a broader term that includes various types of electronic media.

The Editor

An editor is a person responsible for making choices about what and when something appears in a publication. In traditional print publications like a daily newspaper or a monthly magazine, the editor-in-chief is responsible for planning the articles, photographs, visuals, and other content for a particular issue.

Some publications have more than one editor. For example, a metropolitan daily newspaper like the New York Times usually has a sports editor, a business editor, an entertainment editor, a local news editor, a photo editor, a world editor, and other editors responsible for sections of the newspaper. Each editor is responsible for their area, whether in print or online, and they all report to a managing editor called the editor-in-chief.

While some publications have a staff of people who create content, such as authors, photographers, and reporters, other publications operate with just one person, who is both the writer and editor. Many websites, blogs, YouTube channels, and podcasts are written and edited by just one person.

The Schedule

It doesn't matter if the editor is one person or many. A calendar is a valuable tool for planning the work necessary to create the content. With a due date assigned for publishing, it's possible to work backward to determine the tasks needed to make the content and determine the tasks to do the work. If the work is outsourced, the editor knows when to hire and assign the outsourced effort, all in time for the content to be ready on the due date.

An article that requires one week to write can be assigned one week before its due date, and a video that takes a month to produce can be set a month before publication. A photo can be ordered so it's ready on time, whether it takes a few hours to shoot or a few weeks.

The content

While the calendar manages the publication schedule, it also manages what is scheduled. A monthly magazine is an excellent example since it's periodical. Whether online or in print, it still has a date for each issue.

The editor has to choose what goes in each issue. Since content creation takes time, they need to give assignments so there's enough time to prepare it for the publication deadline.

Choosing what goes into each issue is determined by the topics covered by the magazine. A gardening magazine would plan articles for summer issues several months, if not more, in advance. A local newspaper that deals with daily events has to make faster decisions. However, the editor still has to choose what articles appear in print.

Online publications that could publish as soon as something is ready don't always have to do that. They can either release something immediately or hold it for a calendar date. Since there's no need to create a physical form of the media, like a printed copy, online content doesn't require the time to reproduce the printed version.

Even with online sites that create news during the day, some longer lead-time content is usually under development in the editorial calendar. And sometimes, there are not enough articles or content to fill an issue, or an assignment is running late, so editors have backup plans with articles or content that can be ready on short notice.

If you're a blogger, having a few extra pieces on hand is a good idea if you're running late on publishing something in your next issue.

Types of Media

Web pages can display and play text, images, video and audio, making them highly versatile for publications. Fast internet connections have made it easier for users to access larger files that contain audio and video content, so all of these types of content have become more frequently used for publishing on the internet. As a result, there aren't just articles or photos; there's "content."

While it might be technically possible to publish different media types, it's up to the site publisher and editor to decide the media type. Some creators prefer to write blogs, others to post photos, some like videos, while others like to create audio podcasts. The internet makes using any of these and other media types possible. Hence, the only limit is the author's imagination and technical skills.

What should an editorial calendar look like?

If you plan on using an editorial calendar, there's no right or wrong way to do it. Any format can work as long as you have a date and name for your entries. Using the calendar on your computer or mobile smartphone, notes posted on a bulletin board, a journal, or a document are all acceptable ways. Choose a format that is easy to view and update since you'll want to be able to make changes.

If you share your calendar with others, I recommend using a cloud-based calendar like Google Calendar, iCloud, or Microsoft 365, where it's possible to collaborate with a team and share one calendar that can be edited by multiple users.

Readers and viewers

An editorial calendar benefits people who "consume" the content since it can tell them when a particular article, video, or broadcast will be available. Movies use a release calendar for individual pictures, so you'll know when they are available in the theater, magazines announce articles appearing in the next issue, and television series announce their season preview dates. People like to know when something will be ready, especially if they look forward to seeing it.

Next Steps

Next Steps

- Determine your target
- Find a competitor to benchmark
- Focus on one or two social media sites
- Schedule with an editorial calendar
- Manage your time
- Budget for services like post writers and stock photos
- Measure using the analytic tools

Determine Your Target Audience

Knowing as much as possible about your target audience is necessary to determine what content you'll need to create and publish to attract and keep them interested. Without knowing what hobbies, activities, relationships, websites, and other information about your target audience, you only guess what to publish. Remember that people use social media for social activities with their network and that emotional appeal is essential to your content.

There are worksheets at the end of this section you can use to help determine who your perfect target audience is. The more you learn about them, the more you can create engaging social media content.

Find a Competitor to Benchmark

Benchmarking is a process where one organization is compared to others. It's valuable because you can see where you stand in marketing efforts compared to a mother organization that does it well, if not the best. By studying the best, you can learn what they are doing and what you should think about changing to improve. Used by large consulting firms that charge hundreds of dollars an hour for their services, you can do it yourself. Here's how.

Search the web for one or two organizations in the same industry and similar to you. A non-profit with a local focus could look for another local non-profit. A medical practitioner can find someone similar, a realtor, another realtor, etc... Find a business or professional as similar to you as possible. Suppose you were going to start a coffee shop. In that case, you'd probably want to research Starbucks or, if you were going to start an online shopping service, Amazon. The benchmark organization (or person) is good if you say, "I want to be as good as them."

Once you find one or two, study them. Research their website, social media accounts, and other online activity to see what they do. What kinds of posts, how often, the photos they use, offers, and ads. It's OK to follow or like them and even signup for a newsletter. You won't copy their material, but you can learn from their activity. By studying your competition, the competitive research part of marketing, you can see what works for them, then adapt it to your marketing efforts.

Pick One or Two Social Media Sites to Focus

Based on the targeting you did in the previous step, narrow down the social media marketing sites to one or two networks that are used by your target audience. While it may be tempting to start efforts on three or four social media sites to kick-start your marketing, your efforts may become too diluted, and you may not accomplish much. Once you develop a successful formula on one, move on to the next one. You only have to focus on the social media sites used by your target audience. Knowing your target as well as possible will help you save time and focus your efforts.

Schedule Your Content Posting

Make a schedule for your content posting and stick to it using your editorial calendar. If you post once a week, be committed to maintaining that schedule. If you're learning to use social networking sites or tools, give yourself additional time to learn and practice. As you become more familiar with social media, you'll find that creating a post can be done in advance and prepared for posting. Posting doesn't take as long as when you first started.

Allocate Time

Determine how much time you can spend on social media marketing, and determine a timeframe for your efforts. Remember, you may be learning how to use social media sites at the beginning, so give yourself additional time for learning. As you learn, your efforts will become more focused on doing social media marketing, and you'll become more productive. Use an egg timer to set up a time for social media marketing if you don't have one. You can do this in about 15 minutes to a ½ hour per day once you learn how, but be sure to separate your activity as it's easy to get distracted.

Determine Your Budget for Services

If you've decided to spend money on advertising, set a realistic budget that you can use to test several ads or deals, then run them for several weeks or months to see if you have a successful campaign. Also, budget any professional work you may need to hire, such as artwork, photography, websites, or copywriting.

Measure Your Results

After determining goals for the results you want to achieve, make sure you can measure the results. Too often, marketing is done without a review of the results. Measure your results in realistic terms for social media, such as ad clicks, fans, followers, deals, check-ins, reviews, or other measurable items. Don't try to do it all at once since you need to learn if it's new, and you'll have some trial and error as you get feedback on what content goes over well with your target audience. Summary

Regardless of your social networking experience, remember that you are telling a story with your status updates, posts, and profile.

Remember that you don't have to use all of the social networks. Try them on for size and see what fits. Choose the ones used by the people you wish to establish connections with and remember, you will change your activity as you learn more.

ADDITIONAL RESOURCES

Students who attend my class and purchase this book are able to take advantage of all the material available to my limited access membership website for 365 days.

To register and access this content follow these instructions:

1. Go to www.bobology.com

2. Scroll down on your web browser until you see the blue Promo Code box on the right.

3. Enter the promo code **FBMKTG15**

4. Complete the registration form on the next web page

5. Confirm your membership email subscription

6. Log in to the Members only area with your member username and password

With your 365 day access you'll be able to use all of the following:

A Library of How-to articles - articles with how-to instructions, updates on technology, and additional information not included in classes and workbooks.

Technology Explanations - using the same style and approach used in my classes, with clear, easy-to-understand information.

Discussion Forum Moderated by Bob Cohen - answers to *your* questions from Bob and his own advisors in this exclusive members-only forum.

News updates on technology - the latest info in technology from news sources personally selected by Bob.

Plus more:

- **Downloadable Copies of Class Slides**
- **Access to Newsletter Archives**
- **Resource Directory for Solutions**
- **Document and Software Downloads for the class**
- **Updated Social Media Marketing articles only available to members**

www.ingramcontent.com/pod-product-compliance
Lightning Source LLC
LaVergne TN
LVHW060145070326
832902LV00018B/2961

* 9 7 8 1 9 8 1 9 8 4 3 2 9 *